Georgia Evidence Code Handbook

with
Common Objections
&
Evidentiary Foundations

2023

(Rules last amended effective July 2022)

Professor John Barkai

Cover colors are from the Georgia state flag

Regarding copyright – there is none. Of course, there is no claim to copyright the Georgia Evidence Code, a government publication. In addition, I give you permission to freely copy and use other sections of this handbook, including the sections on objections and evidentiary foundations, under a Creative Commons Attribution (CCBY) 4.0 License, which essentially means that you may use, share, or adapt the information in these pages for any purpose, even commercial, if you give "appropriate credit" and indicate changes you made, if any. Please cite the material as: John Barkai, Georgia Evidence Code Handbook with Common Objections & Evidentiary Foundations. Also, you cannot restrict others from using these materials.

Formatting. There is no standard formatting style for presenting rules of evidence. This handbook uses formatting intended to make the understanding and application of the rules as clear as possible - but clarity and ease of understanding of the rules of evidence by using the text alone is almost impossible. Fonts vary, using larger fonts for rules you are likely to consult more often, and smaller fonts for rules less likely consulted. Some words are underlined for emphasis.

Disclaimer: The author is not offering legal advice. Your trial judge may view the law and foundations differently. The law is whatever the judge in your case says it is. Any errors in this book are mine.

Corrections, omissions, suggestions?
See any or have some? Contact me at barkai@hawaii.edu

Common Citation Forms for the Georgia rules:
  Official Code of Georgia Annotated (O.C.G.A.) Title 24

  O.C.G.A. § 24-X-XXX, or even GRE or Ga. E. C. xxx.

Rules last amended: 24-7-702 effective July 2022;
24-4-412. 24-4-419, 24-5-510 effective in 2021.

Georgia Evidence Code Handbook
with Common Objections & Evidentiary Foundations

Professor John Barkai
William S. Richardson School of Law
University of Hawaii
Honolulu, HI 96822
Jan. 2023

ISBN: 9798536466025

INTRODUCTION

This handbook of the Georgia Evidence Code was designed to be brought to court and be at your side in the office.

Besides the Georgia rules of evidence, the **"added value"** in this handbook is the following useful and entertaining sections:

A) **Making and Responding to Common Objections** (16 pages)
   A list and discussion of the most common objections.

B) **Evidentiary Foundations and Impeachment** (over 60 pages)
   More than 25 examples of the most common evidentiary foundations and a brief discussion of differing standards for authenticating digital evidence (such as email, text messages, social media sites, and internet sites)

The sample foundation and impeachment questions are "bare-bones" foundations which include the minimum questions and answers necessary to get testimony or exhibits admitted into evidence

Professor John Barkai

SUMMARY OF CONTENTS

Introduction iii
Summary of Contents iv
Expanded Table of Contents v
Sample Pages from Deeper in the Handbook viii
Georgia Evidence Code (by number and title) xiii
Most Commonly Used Hearsay Sub-Sections xviii
Georgia Evidence Code (full rules) 1-86

Appendix

Making and Responding to Common Objections .... A - 1
    A List of Common Objections A-16
Evidentiary Foundations **A-17**
    Sample Foundational Questions (Predicates) A-34
    Digital Evidence – Electronically Stored Information – ESI . A-61

Books by John Barkai A-76
History and Restyling of the Federal Rules of Evidence A-78
Dedication A-79
About the Author A-79

Expanded Appendix
Making and Responding to Common Objections A-1
Why Do Lawyers Object?..A-1
Make an Objection in Four Steps A-2
How to Respond to an Objection A-2
If You are a Judge Who Has to Rule on the Objection....................A-3
Multiple Lawyers and Multiple Clients A-3
Judges Apply the Rules of Evidence More Loosely in Nonjury Trials. A-3
The Key to Objections is Rule 103 ....A-3
Important Points about Rule 103 ....A-4
Rule 103. Rulings on Evidence...A-4
Objections - Rules - Constitutional Issues A-5
Motions in Limine A-5
Phrases that Suggest Inadmissible Information A-6
Inadequate Objections A-6
Offers of Proof A-6
Nonjury Trials – Seldom Reversed A-7
Common Phrases from Court Opinions...A-7
Common Objections to the Form of the Question A-8
    Argumentative (Harassing, Badgering) A-8
    Asked and Answered A-8
    Assuming Facts Not in Evidence. A-9
    Beyond the Scope A-9
    Compound Question. A-10
    Cumulative A-10
    Lack of Foundation A-10
    Leading Question A-11
    Motion to strike A-11
    Narrative Question A-12
    Non-Responsive Answer A-12
    Speculation..A-13
    Vague and Ambiguous Question A-13
    Golden Rule A-13
    Speaking Objections A-14
    Coaching the Witness A-14
    Relevance A-14
    A Few Useful Definitions A-15
    Stipulation A-15
    Offer of Proof..A-15
    Motion in Limine A-15
    Limited Admissibility A-15
    Intrinsic Impeachment A-15
    Extrinsic A-15
    Collateral A-15
A List of Common Objections...A-16

Evidentiary Foundations...A-17
Foundations – Laying the Foundation - Predicates........................A-17
Bare-Bones Foundations A-18
Admissibility v. Weight A-19
Example of Admissibility and Weight A-19
3 Simple Questions A-20
Steps for Introducing Exhibits A-21
The Common Evidentiary Foundations A-23
Phrases to Move Evidence into a Trial A-24
Useful Points to Remember A-25
Offering Something into Evidence A-25
Make an Offer of Proof A-25
Hearsay Within Hearsay A-25
Public Records Do Not Have to Be Open to The Public A-25
Computer Generated Record are not Hearsay A-25
Emails Offered to Show Notice, Knowledge or Fear Are Not Hearsay A-25
Demonstrative Evidence A-25
Chain of Custody A-25
Distinctive Characteristics A-25
Authenticate with Personal Knowledge and Distinctive Characteristics....A-26
Affidavits Are Hearsay and Inadmissible at Trial A-26
HARROWing A-26
OTP – Offered to Prove A-26
Rules Do Not Explain How to Introduce Evidence in Court A-26
Laying A Foundation is Like a Sport A-26
Mark, Show, Approach, Foundational Questions, Offer A-26
Magic Words A-27
Speak in Generic Terms A-27
"Publish" Means to Show the exhibit Now A-27
Chain of Custody Is Only for Fungible Items or Samples to Test A-27
Basic Tasks a Trial Lawyer Should Be Able to Do.........................A-27
Best Evidentiary Foundation Resources A-27
Important Evidence Rules to Guide You R 103, 104, 901, 612, 613, 801, 803(6), 901, 902(11), 902(13&14), 105, 106, 1006 ....A-28
Opponent Has the Burden on the Issue of Trustworthiness A-29
Basic Foundation and Impeachment Examples A-30
NITA Liquor Commission Facts A-31
Officer Bier's Report A-32
Diagram of Cut-Rate Liquor Store Area A-33
Photograph of a Scene A-34
Diagram of the Scene A-35
Real Evidence – Thunderbird Wine Bottle......................................A-36
Offering a Contract into Evidence...A-37
Refreshing Memory with Anything..A-38

Writing Used to Refresh Memory – R612 .... A-40
Refreshing Memory with a Leading Question A-41
Recorded Recollection (Author's Rule) A-42
Business Records - Custodian of Records – R803(6)....................... A-44
Business Records Are KRAP A-45
Self-Authenticating Business Records Form - Texas A-46
Demonstrative Evidence - Similar to the Real Item A-47
Impeachment - Prior Written Inconsistent Statement A-48
Impeachment - Omission A-50
Impeachment - Inconsistent Oral Deposition A-52
Impeachment - Inconsistent Oral Deposition - Short Form A-53
Impeachment - Inconsistent Oral Deposition - Long Form............ A-54
Impeachment - Inconsistent Oral Statement A-55
Using Learned Treatises A-56
Learned Treatises Use on Direct Exam – R803(18) A-57
Learned Treatises: Use on Cross – R803(18) A-58
Voicemail and Phone Conversations A-59
Digital Evidence – Electronically Stored Information – ESI A-61
A Variety of Different Standards.. A-61
Distinctive Characteristics and Circumstantial Evidence A-63
Presenting Digital Evidence from a Cell Phone in Court A-64
Digital Evidence and Self-Authentication A-65
Digital Evidence Foundations A-66
Email – Outgoing A-66
Email – Incoming A-67
Text Message – Received by Witness A-68
Social Media: Facebook, Instagram, Snapchat, Twitter A-69
Internet Website – Web Posting A-70
Fax – Incoming A-71
Foundation for Expert Opinion A-72
Books by John Barkai A-76
History and Restyling of the Federal Rules of Evidence A-78
Dedication A-79
About the Author A-79

SAMPLE PAGE FROM DEEPER IN THE HANDBOOK

Make an Objection in Four Steps
1) Stand up.
2) Say, "Objection _____ " (Fill in the blank with your reason).
3) Identify your specific objection.
    a) At a minimum, say the topic type
        (Hearsay, Relevance, Improper Impeachment, Improper Character, Lack of Foundation, Leading Question, etc.)
    b) State the evidence rule number if you know it (404, 608, etc.).
    c) A combination of the above
        ("Objection, Improper Impeachment, R613")
4) Stop talking and listen to the judge.
Be prepared to state reasons for your objection and to make an argument to support your position.

How to Respond to An Objection
1) Speak to the judge, not the lawyer who objected.
2) Explain to the judge why your evidence should be admissible. ("Your Honor, that statement is not hearsay because I am not offering it for the truth but rather to show notice.")
3) If you recognize that you did not lay an appropriate foundation for the evidence explain that you will do that. ("Your Honor, I will lay the foundation.")
4) If you recognize that the opposing counsel was objecting to the form of your question, which most often happens on your direct examination, simply say, "I'll rephrase." Rephrase the question and move on with your witness examination. Do not get sidetracked by the opposing counsel who might have objected just to throw you off track.
5) For any physical piece of evidence, statement, or testimony that you will be introducing, prepare in advance and have a reason why you believe that evidence is admissible. Be ready to make that argument to the judge.
6) If the objection is to relevance, and you think you will be able to show that it is relevant, say to the judge "I will connect it up in a few questions Your Honor." Such a statement is equivalent of saying "trust me." If you do that, you'd better connect it up or the judge will not trust you in the future.

SAMPLE PAGE FROM DEEPER IN THE HANDBOOK

A List of Common Possible Objections

Ambiguous	Improper opinion
Argumentative	Improper rehabilitation
Asked and answered	Inadmissible opinion
Assumes facts not in evidence	Incompetent witness
Authentication	Incomplete Inflammatory
Badgering	Insufficient foundation
Best evidence	Irrelevant (Relevance)
Beyond the scope	Lack of foundation
Bias	Lack of personal knowledge
Bolstering	Leading question
Calls for a conclusion	Misleading
Calls for speculation	Misquotes a witness or exhibit
Chain of custody	Misquotes evidence
Collateral	Misstates witness
Competence	More prejudicial than probative
Compound question	Motion to strike
Compromise / Settlement offer	Narrative
Confrontation (lack of)	(Question calls for a narrative)
Confusing	Narrative answer
Counsel is testifying	Non-responsive
Cumulative	Nothing pending
Document speaks for itself	Outside the scope of cross
Expert (Improper opinion)	Overly broad or general
Expert (not qualified)	Parole evidence rule
Habit	Personal knowledge
Harassing the witness	Prejudice (unfair)
Hearsay	Privilege communication
Hypothetical question misused	Relevance
Improper character evidence	Speculation/ Opinion/ Lack of personal knowledge
Improper characterization	Unintelligible
Improper impeachment	Vague

There are many more possible objections,
limited only by the lawyer's imagination.

Judges and the local legal culture in your jurisdiction may have other rules or approaches to objections that are not touched on in this handbook. Ask around and learn about them.

SAMPLE PAGE FROM DEEPER IN THE HANDBOOK
Steps for Introducing Exhibits

> **Preliminary steps are:**
> 1) **Have the exhibit marked for identification**
> 2) **Show the proposed exhibit to opposing counsel**
> 3) **Ask permission to approach the witness with the proposed exhibit**

1. **History - How the witness knows the exhibit.**
   Offer some testimony that the witness <u>knows</u> or is <u>familiar with</u> the evidence – such as a document, physical item, photo, diagram, scene, text message, email - or recalls the statement. Even if the witness has only seen the exhibit once before or has just been to the scene shown in the photograph once before, <u>once is enough</u>.

2. **The Litany (a ritualistic repetition of foundational questions)**
   a) Ask the court clerk to **mark the item** (using numbers or letters). The clerk will decide which system to use. In more serious cases in the jurisdiction's higher courts (typically where jury trials are allowed), exhibits are usually required to be marked at least before trial starts, and often during pretrial conferences.
   b) **Show opposing counsel** (this will prevent interruptions) and say, "Let the record reflect that I am showing the defense what has been marked as plaintiff's proposed exhibit number one."
   c) Ask the judge for **permission to approach** the witness. "May I approach the witness?"
   - Q: "**I show you what has been marked as** Plaintiff's (Prosecution's) (Defense's) proposed exhibit # x (or exhibit #x for identification purposes) **and ask whether you can identify it**" (You expect a "yes" answer here.)
   - Q: "**What is it?**" (They describe it in general terms. "It is the contract/photo of the scene/weapon recovered/drugs seized/diagram of the area/etc.")
   - Q: "**How do you know that?**" (They answer – "I recognize it. It has my signature on it. / I have been there many times before. / I put my initials on it and the defendant's name/etc.")

SAMPLE PAGE FROM DEEPER IN THE HANDBOOK

3. Show Condition or Comparison or Accuracy

Some comparison must be made between the exhibit in court and when the witness became familiar with the exhibit out-of-court. Of the examples that follow, only one such question is necessary.

- "Is this in the **same** condition as when you... [first saw it...seized it...etc.]?"
- "Is this in the **same or substantially** the same condition.... as when you…" (for item or document)
- "Is it a **fair and accurate representation** of the ... **as it was that day**?" (for diagram or pictures)
- "**Has it changed** in any significant way?"
- "**How does it compare** to the item you saw that day?"

4. Move or Offer the Exhibit into Evidence

"Your honor, **I offer the exhibit into evidence**." - or, "I move the exhibit into evidence."

You could instead say, "I offer proposed exhibit # 1 into evidence as exhibit # 1," but why make it so confusing? Just say, "I offer the exhibit into evidence."

The judge <u>might</u> ask the opposing counsel, "Any objections?" but the opponent should object immediately after the proponent offers the exhibit if there is an objection to the admissibility (not the weight). The judge should allow "voir dire" (immediate cross examination limited to the foundation and the admissibility) by the opponent of the exhibit.

SAMPLE PAGE FROM DEEPER IN THE HANDBOOK

Authentication of Text Message – An Example

Text Message

Received by Witness

Do you know Y?

Do you communicate with Y on a regular basis?

In what ways to you communicate with Y?

Did you receive a text message from the Y [recently; on or about _ date, on the topic of ..., etc.]?

Would you recognize a printout of the message if you were to see it again?

Let me show you what has been marked as proposed exhibit # 1. Do you recognize it?

What is it? [Ans: A screenshot from my cell phone]

How do you know that this is a message from Y? [It is similar to other messages I have received from Y in that ...]

How did it appear when it arrived on your phone? [Showed up under the name and with the picture I had previously assigned to Y]

What other distinctive characteristics did you notice about the message? [provide as many as distinctive characteristics possible]

Is it a fair and accurate representation of the text message you received [recently; on or about _ date, on the topic of visiting your son, etc.]?

Has it been altered in any way?

I would like to enter the proposed exhibit into evidence

Georgia Evidence Code

Official Code of Georgia Annotated (O.C.G.A.) Title 24
(Rules last amended and effective July 2022)

Chapter 1 General Provisions
Article 1 Purpose and Applicability of Rules of Evidence.
Sec.
24-1-1. Purpose and construction of the rules of evidence. 1
24-1-2. Applicability of the rules of evidence. 1
Article 2 General Evidentiary Matters.
24-1-101. Reserved. 2
24-1-102. Reserved. 2
24-1-103. Rulings on evidence. 2
24-1-104. Preliminary questions. 3
24-1-105. Limited admissibility. 3
24-1-106. Introduction of remaining portions of writings or recorded statements. 3

Chapter 2 Judicial Notice
Article 1 Adjudicative Facts.
24-2-201. Judicial notice of adjudicative facts. 4
Article 2 Legislative Facts; Ordinances or Resolutions.
24-2-220. Judicial notice of legislative facts. 4
24-2-221. Judicial notice of ordinance or resolution. 4

Chapter 3 Parol Evidence
24-3-1. Parol evidence contradicting writing inadmissible generally. 5
24-3-2. Proof of unwritten portions of contract admissible where not inconsistent. 5
24-3-3. Contemporaneous writings explaining each other; parol evidence explaining ambiguities. 5
24-3-4. Circumstances surrounding execution of contracts. 5
24-3-5. Known usage. 5
24-3-6. Rebuttal of equity; discharge of contract; proof of subsequent agreement; change of time or place of performance. 5
24-3-7. Proof of mistake in deed or written contract. 5
24-3-8. Original or subsequent voidness of writing. 5
24-3-9. Explanation or denial of receipts. 5
24-3-10. Explanation of blank endorsements. 5

Chapter 4 Relevant Evidence and Its Limits
24-4-401. "Relevant evidence" defined. 6
24-4-402. Relevant evidence generally admissible; irrelevant evidence not admissible. ... 6
24-4-403. Exclusion of relevant evidence on the grounds of prejudice, confusion, or waste of time. 6
24-4-404. Character evidence not admissible to prove conduct; exceptions; other crimes. 6
24-4-405. Methods of proving character. 7
24-4-406. Habit; routine practice. 7
24-4-407. Subsequent remedial measures. 7
24-4-408. Compromises and offers to compromise. 7
24-4-409. Payment of medical and similar expenses. 8
24-4-410. Inadmissibility of pleas, plea discussions, and related statements. 8
24-4-411. Liability insurance. 8
24-4-412. Complainant's past sexual behavior not admissible in prosecutions for certain sexual offenses; exceptions. 9
24-4-413. Evidence of similar transaction crimes in sexual assault cases. 10
24-4-414. Evidence of similar transaction crimes in child molestation cases. 10
24-4-415. Evidence of similar acts in civil or administrative proceedings concerning sexual assault or child molestation. 11
24-4-416. Statements of sympathy in medical malpractice cases. 12
24-4-417. Evidence of similar acts in prosecutions for violations of Code Section 40-6-391. 12
24-4-418. Admissibility of criminal gang activity, disclosure. 13

Chapter 5 Privileges

- 24-5-501. Certain communications privileged. ...14
- 24-5-502. Communications to clergyman privileged. ...14
- 24-5-503. Husband and wife as witnesses for and against each other in criminal proceedings. ...15
- 24-5-504. Law enforcement officers testifying; home address. ...15
- 24-5-505. Party or witness privilege. ...15
- 24-5-506. Privilege against self-incrimination; testimony of accused in criminal case. ...15
- 24-5-507. Grant of immunity; contempt. ...16
- 24-5-508. Qualified privilege for news gathering or dissemination. ...16
- 24-5-509. Communications between victim of family violence or sexual assault and agents providing services to such victim; termination of privilege. ...17
- 24-5-510. Privileged communications between law enforcement officers and peer counselors. ...19

Chapter 6 Witnesses
Article 1 General Provisions.

- 24-6-601. General rule of competency. ...20
- 24-6-602. Lack of personal knowledge. ...20
- 24-6-603. Oath or affirmation. ...20
- 24-6-604. Interpreters. ...20
- 24-6-605. Judge as witness. ...20
- 24-6-606. Juror as witness. ...20
- 24-6-607. Who may impeach. ...21
- 24-6-608. Evidence of character and conduct of witness. ...21
- 24-6-609. Impeachment by evidence of conviction of a crime. ...22
- 24-6-610. Religious beliefs or opinions. ...23
- 24-6-611. Mode and order of witness interrogation and presentation. ...23
- 24-6-612. Writing used to refresh memory. ...23
- 24-6-613. Prior statements of witnesses. ...24
- 24-6-614. Calling and interrogation of witnesses by court. ...24
- 24-6-615. Exclusion of witnesses. ...24
- 24-6-616. Presence in courtroom of victim of criminal offense. ...24

Article 2 Credibility.

- 24-6-620. Credibility a jury question. ...25
- 24-6-621. Impeachment by contradiction. ...25
- 24-6-622. Witness's feelings and relationship to parties provable. ...25
- 24-6-623. Treatment of witness. ...25

Article 3 Use of Sign Language and Intermediary Interpreter in Administrative and Judicial Proceedings.

- 24-6-650. State policy on hearing impaired persons. ...25
- 24-6-651. Definitions. ...25
- 24-6-652. Appointment of interpreters for hearing impaired persons interested in or witness at agency proceedings. ...26
- 24-6-653. Procedure for interrogation and taking of statements from hearing impaired persons arrested for violation of criminal laws. ...26
- 24-6-654. Indigent hearing impaired defendants to be provided with interpreters. ...26
- 24-6-655. Waiver of right to interpreter. ...27
- 24-6-656. Replacement of interpreters unable to communicate accurately with hearing impaired persons; appointment of intermediary interpreters. ...27
- 24-6-657. Oath of interpreters; privileged communications; taping and filming of hearing impaired persons' testimony. ...27
- 24-6-658. Compensation of interpreters. ...27

Chapter 7 Opinions and Expert Testimony

- 24-7-701. Lay witness opinion testimony. ...28
- 24-7-702. Expert opinion testimony in civil actions; medical experts; pretrial hearings; precedential value of federal law. ...28
- 24-7-703. Bases of expert opinion testimony. ...30
- 24-7-704. Ultimate issue opinion. ...30
- 24-7-705. Disclosure of facts or data underlying expert opinion. ...30
- 24-7-706. Court appointed experts. ...31
- 24-7-707. Expert opinion testimony in criminal proceedings. ...31

Chapter 8 Hearsay
Article 1 General Provisions.
24-8-801. Definitions. ...32
24-8-802. Hearsay rule. ...33
24-8-803. Hearsay rule exceptions; availability of declarant immaterial. ...33
24-8-804. Hearsay rule exceptions; declarant unavailable. ...36
24-8-805. Hearsay within hearsay. ...37
24-8-806. Attacking and supporting credibility of a declarant. ...37
24-8-807. Residual exception. ...38
Article 2 Admissions and Confessions.
24-8-820. Testimony as to child's description of sexual contact or physical abuse. ...38
24-8-821. Admissions in pleadings. ...38
24-8-822. Right to have whole conversation heard. ...38
24-8-823. Admissions and confessions received with care; no conviction on uncorroborated confession. ...38
24-8-824. Only voluntary confessions admissible. ...39
24-8-825. Confessions under spiritual exhortation, promise of secrecy, or collateral benefit admissible. ...39
24-8-826. Medical reports in narrative form. ...39
Chapter 9 Authentication and Identification
Article 1 General Provisions.
24-9-901. Requirement of authentication or identification. ...40
24-9-902. Self-authentication. ...41
24-9-903. Subscribing witness's testimony. ...42
24-9-904. Definitions. ...42
Article 2 Specific Types of Records and Evidence.
24-9-920. Authentication of Georgia state and county records. ...43
24-9-921. Identification of medical bills; expert witness unnecessary. ...43
24-9-922. Proof of laws, records, nonjudicial records, or books of other states, territories, or possessions; full faith and credit. ...43
24-9-923. Authentication of photographs, motion pictures, video recordings, and audio recordings when witness unavailable. ...44
24-9-924. Admissibility of records of Department of Driver Services; admissibility of computer transmitted records. ...44
Chapter 10 Best Evidence Rule
24-10-1001. Definitions. ...45
24-10-1002. Requirement of original. ...45
24-10-1003. Admissibility of duplicates. ...45
24-10-1004. Admissibility of other evidence of contents of a writing, recording, or photograph. ...45
24-10-1005. Public records. ...46
24-10-1006. Summaries. ...46
24-10-1007. Testimony or written admission of party. ...46
24-10-1008. Functions of court and jury. ...46
Chapter 11 Establishment of Lost Records
Article 1 Public Records.
24-11-1. Definitions. ...46
24-11-2. Establishment of lost records. ...47
24-11-3. Appointment of auditor; hearing; establishment of duplicates. ...47
Article 2 Private Papers.
24-11-20. Establishment of lost office papers. ...47
24-11-21. Summary establishment of lost or destroyed evidence of indebtedness in probate court – Petition; service of notice; hearing and decision; recordation; appeal to superior court. ...48
24-11-22. Summary establishment of lost or destroyed evidence of indebtedness in probate court – Service of nonresidents; effect. ...49
24-11-23. Establishment of lost or destroyed paper in superior court - Petition and affidavit; issuance and service of rule nisi. ...49
24-11-24. Establishment of lost or destroyed paper in superior court - When continuance granted. ...49
24-11-25. Establishment of lost or destroyed paper. ...49
24-11-26. Establishment of lost or destroyed paper - Furnishing of certified endorsement of copy. ...49
24-11-27. Procedure as to action on lost or destroyed note, bill, bond, or other instrument. ...50
24-11-28. Joinder of additional party defendants in proceedings to establish lost or destroyed papers. 50
24-11-29. Applicability of article. ...50

Chapter 12 Medical and other Confidential Information
Article 1 Release of Medical Information and Confidentiality of Raw Research Data.
24-12-1. When medical information may be released by physician, hospital, health care facility, or pharmacist; immunity from liability; waiver of privilege; psychiatrists and hospitals excepted. 51
24-12-2. Confidentiality of raw research data. 52
Article 2 Confidentiality of Medical Information.
24-12-10. Definitions. 53
24-12-11. Disclosure of medical records - Effect on confidential or privileged character thereof. 53
24-12-12. Disclosure of medical records - Use of medical matter disclosed. 55
24-12-13. Disclosure of medical records - Immunity from liability. 55
24-12-14. Disclosure of medical records - Use for educational purposes not precluded. 55
Article 3 AIDS Information.
24-12-20. Confidential nature of AIDS information. 55
24-12-21. Disclosure of AIDS confidential information. 55
Article 4 Other Confidential Information.
24-12-30. Confidential nature of certain library records. 63
24-12-31. Confidential nature of veterinarian records; disclosure of rabies vaccination record. 64

Chapter 13 Securing Attendance of Witnesses and Production and Preservation of Evidence
Article 1 General Provisions.
24-13-1. Freedom of witnesses from arrest. 64
24-13-2. Procedure for claiming witness fees. 64
24-13-3. Witness fee exceptions. 64
24-13-4. Penalty for excessive witness fee claim. 65
24-13-5. Production of evidence when item not available; oath. 65
24-13-6. Procedure when adverse party dissatisfied with response pursuant to Code Section 24-13-5. 65
24-13-7. Withdrawal of originals introduced in evidence; substitution of copies; discretion of court. .65
Article 2 Subpoenas and Notice to Produce.
24-13-20. Applicability. 66
24-13-21. Subpoena for attendance of witnesses - Form; issuance; subpoena in blank. 66
24-13-22. Subpoena for attendance of witnesses - Attendance at hearing or trial; where served. 66
24-13-23. Subpoena for production of documentary evidence; motion to quash or modify. 66
24-13-24. Service of subpoenas. 67
24-13-25. Fees and mileage; when tender required. 67
24-13-26. Enforcement of subpoenas; continuance; secondary evidence of books, papers, or documents. 67
24-13-27. Notice to produce. 67
24-13-28. Witness fees for law enforcement officers. 68
24-13-29. Legislators' exemption. 69
Article 3 Securing Attendance of Prisoners.
24-13-60. Order requiring prisoner's delivery to serve as witness or criminal defendant generally; expenses; prisoner under death sentence as witness. 70
24-13-61. Issuance of order requiring prisoner's delivery to serve as witness in superior court. 70
24-13-62. Issuance of writ of habeas corpus requiring prisoner's delivery to serve as witness in superior court. 71
Article 4 Uniform Act to Secure the Attendance of Witnesses from Without the State.
24-13-90. Short title. 71
24-13-91. Definitions. 71
24-13-92. Criminal or grand jury proceeding in foreign state - Certificate of need for testimony; expenses; punishment. 72
24-13-93. Criminal or grand jury proceeding in foreign state - Certificate of need for prisoner's testimony; order by judge in requesting state; applicability. 73
24-13-94. Criminal or grand jury proceeding in this state - Issuance of certificate; how long witness detained; punishment. 74
24-13-95. Criminal or grand jury proceeding in this state - Issuance of certificate seeking testimony of prisoner; notice to attorney general; order of compliance. 74
24-13-96. Exemption of witnesses from arrest and service of process. 75
24-13-97. Construction. 75

Article 5 Uniform Interstate Depositions and Discovery Act.
24-13-110. Short title. 75
24-13-111. Definitions. 75
24-13-112. Requirements for issuance of foreign subpoenas; application. 76
24-13-113. Compelling foreign witness to appear and testify. 76
24-13-114. Service of foreign subpoena. 76
24-13-115. Applicability of Article 2 to certain provisions of this article. 76
24-13-116. Protective order or enforcement, quashing, or modification of foreign subpoena. ...76

Article 6 Depositions to Preserve Testimony in Criminal Proceedings.
24-13-130. When deposition to preserve testimony in criminal proceedings may be taken. 77
24-13-131. Notice of deposition; presence of defendant at examination; child witness. 78
24-13-132. Appointment of counsel; payment of costs and expenses. 79
24-13-133. Manner of taking and filing deposition. 79
24-13-134. Availability to state and defendant of deponent's previous statements. 79
24-13-135. Admissibility and use of deposition. 79
24-13-136. Objections to admission of deposition. 80
24-13-137. Recordation of deposition. 80
24-13-138. Agreement of parties to deposition. 80
24-13-139. Depositions taken only in exceptional circumstances; misuse of procedures. 80

Article 7 Perpetuation of Testimony.
24-13-150. When proceedings to perpetuate testimony may be had. 80
24-13-151. Inadequacy of usual proceeding to be shown. 80
24-13-152. Materiality of possession of property; of availability of parties in interest. 81
24-13-153. Use of testimony. 81
24-13-154. Costs of proceedings. 81

Chapter 14 Proof Generally
Article 1 General Provisions.
24-14-1. On whom burden of proof lies. 81
24-14-2. Change of burden in discretion of court. 81
24-14-3. Amount of mental conviction required; preponderance of evidence in civil cases. 81
24-14-4. Determining where preponderance of evidence lies. 81
24-14-5. Reasonable doubt in criminal cases. 82
24-14-6. When conviction may be had on circumstantial evidence. 82
24-14-7. Positive testimony preferred over negative; exception. 82
24-14-8. Number of witnesses required generally; exceptions; effect of corroboration. 82
24-14-9. Inferences from evidence or lack thereof. 82

Article 2 Presumptions and Estoppel.
24-14-20. Presumptions of law and of fact distinguished. 82
24-14-21. Rebuttable presumptions of law. 82
24-14-22. Presumption from failure to produce evidence. 83
24-14-23. Presumption from failure to answer business letter. 83
24-14-24. Presumption of occupancy of railroad right of way. 83
24-14-25. Presumption of payment of check. 83
24-14-26. Estoppels defined; enumeration generally. 84
24-14-27. Estoppel relating to real estate. 84
24-14-28. Trustees estopped to set up title adverse to trust. 84
24-14-29. Equitable estoppel. 84

Article 3 Particular Matters of Proof.
24-14-40. Evidence of identity; burden in civil proceedings. 85
24-14-41. Proof of de facto officer. 85
24-14-42. Judgment admissible; effect. 85
24-14-43. Calendars as proof of dates. 85
24-14-44. American Experience Mortality Tables. 85
24-14-45. Other mortality tables. 85
24-14-46. United States Department of Agriculture inspection certificates prima-facie evidence. 86
24-14-47. Proof that person is dead or missing as evidence. 86

The Most Commonly Used Georgia Hearsay Sub-Sections

§ 24-8-801. Definitions 32
    (a) Statement 32
    (b) Declarant 32
    (c) Hearsay 32
    (d)(1) Prior Statement by witness 32
        (A) (inconsistent or consistent statement) 32
        (B) (to impeach or rehabilitate) 32
        (C) (prior identification) 32
    (2) Admission by party-opponent 32

§ 24-8-802. Hearsay Rule 33

§ 24-8-803. Hearsay rule exceptions; availability of declarant immaterial 33
    (1) Present sense impression 33
    (2) Excited utterance 33
    (3) Then existing mental, emotional, or physical condition 33
    (4) Statements for purposes of medical diagnosis or treatment 33
    (5) Recorded recollection 34
    (6) Records of regularly conducted activity (business records) 34
    (8) Public records and reports 34
    (17) Market reports and commercial publications 35
    (18) Learned treatises 35

§ 24-8-804. Hearsay rule exceptions; declarant unavailable 36
    804(b)
    (1) [former testimony] 37
    (2) [dying declaration] 37
    (3) Statement against interest 37

§ 24-8-5. Hearsay within hearsay 37

Georgia Evidence Code

Chapter 1. General Provisions
Article 1. Purpose And Applicability of Rules of Evidence

§ 24-1-1. Purpose and construction of the rules of evidence

The object of all legal investigation is the discovery of truth. Rules of evidence shall be construed to secure fairness in administration, eliminate unjustifiable expense and delay, and promote the growth and development of the law of evidence to the end that the truth may be ascertained and proceedings justly determined.

§ 24-1-2. Applicability of the rules of evidence

(a) The rules of evidence shall apply in all trials by jury in any court in this state.
(b) The rules of evidence shall apply generally to all nonjury trials and other fact-finding proceedings of any court in this state subject to the limitations set forth in subsections (c) and (d) of this Code section.
(c) The rules of evidence, except those with respect to privileges, shall not apply in the following situations:
    (1) The determination of questions of fact preliminary to admissibility of evidence when the issue is to be determined by the court under Code Section 24-1-104;
    (2) Criminal proceedings before grand juries;
    (3) Proceedings for extradition or rendition;
    (4) Proceedings for revoking parole;
    (5) Proceedings for the issuance of warrants for arrest and search warrants except as provided by subsection (b) of Code Section 17-4-40;
    (6) Proceedings with respect to release on bond;
    (7) Dispositional hearings and custody hearings in juvenile court; or
    (8) Contempt proceedings in which the court, pursuant to subsection (a) of Code Section 15-1-4, may act summarily.
(d)
    (1) In criminal commitment or preliminary hearings in any court, the rules of evidence shall apply except that hearsay shall be admissible.
    (2) In in rem forfeiture proceedings, the rules of evidence shall apply except that hearsay shall be admissible in determining probable cause or reasonable cause.
    (3) In presentence hearings, the rules of evidence shall apply except that hearsay and character evidence shall be admissible.
    (4) In administrative hearings, the rules of evidence as applied in the trial of nonjury civil actions shall be followed, subject to special statutory rules or agency rules as authorized by law.
(e) Except as modified by statute, the common law as expounded by Georgia courts shall continue to be applied to the admission and exclusion of evidence and to procedures at trial.

Article 2. General Evidentiary Matters

§ 24-1-101. Reserved

§ 24-1-102. Reserved

§ 24-1-103. Rulings on evidence
(a) Error shall not be predicated upon a ruling which admits or excludes evidence unless a substantial right of the party is affected and:
  (1) In case the ruling is one admitting evidence, a timely objection or motion to strike appears of record, stating the specific ground of objection, if the specific ground was not apparent from the context; or
  (2) In case the ruling is one excluding evidence, the substance of the evidence was made known to the court by an offer of proof or was apparent from the context within which questions were asked.
Once the court makes a definitive ruling on the record admitting or excluding any evidence, either at or before trial, a party need not renew an objection or offer of proof to preserve such claim of error for appeal.
(b) The court shall accord the parties adequate opportunity to state grounds for objections and present offers of proof. The court may add any other or further statement which shows the character of the evidence, the form in which it was offered, the objection made, and the ruling thereon. The court may direct the making of an offer of proof in question and answer form.
(c) Jury proceedings shall be conducted, to the extent practicable, so as to prevent inadmissible evidence from being suggested to the jury by any means, including, but not limited to, making statements or offers of proof or asking questions in the hearing of the jury.
(d) Nothing in this Code section shall preclude a court from taking notice of plain errors affecting substantial rights although such errors were not brought to the attention of the court.

§ 24-1-104. Preliminary questions

(a) Preliminary questions concerning the qualification of a person to be a witness, the existence of a privilege, or the admissibility of evidence shall be determined by the court, subject to the provisions of subsection (b) of this Code section. In making its determination, the court shall not be bound by the rules of evidence except those with respect to privileges. Preliminary questions shall be resolved by a preponderance of the evidence standard.

(b) When the relevancy of evidence depends upon the fulfillment of a condition of fact, the court shall admit it upon, or subject to, the introduction of evidence sufficient to support a finding of the fulfillment of the condition.

(c) Hearings on the admissibility of confessions shall in all cases be conducted out of the hearing of the jury. Hearings on other preliminary matters shall be conducted out of the hearing of the jury when the interests of justice require or when an accused is a witness and requests a hearing outside the presence of the jury.

(d) The accused shall not, by testifying upon a preliminary matter, become subject to cross-examination as to other issues in the proceeding.

(e) This Code section shall not limit the right of a party to introduce before the jury evidence relevant to weight or credibility.

§ 24-1-105. Limited admissibility

When evidence which is admissible as to one party or for one purpose but which is not admissible as to another party or for another purpose is admitted, the court, upon request, shall restrict the evidence to its proper scope and instruct the jury accordingly.

§ 24-1-106. Introduction of remaining portions of writings or recorded statements

When a writing or recorded statement or part thereof is introduced by a party, an adverse party may require the introduction at that time of any other part or any other writing or recorded statement which, in fairness, should be considered contemporaneously with the writing or recorded statement.

Chapter 2. Judicial Notice

Article 1. Adjudicative Facts
§ 24-2-201. Judicial notice of adjudicative facts
(a) This Code section governs only judicial notice of adjudicative facts.
(b) A judicially noticed fact shall be a fact which is not subject to reasonable dispute in that it is either:
    (1) Generally known within the territorial jurisdiction of the court; or
    (2) Capable of accurate and ready determination by resort to sources whose accuracy cannot reasonably be questioned.
(c) A court may take judicial notice, whether or not requested by a party.
(d) A court shall take judicial notice if requested by a party and provided with the necessary information.
(e) A party shall be entitled, upon timely request, to an opportunity to be heard as to the propriety of taking judicial notice and the tenor of the matter noticed. In the absence of prior notification, such request may be made after judicial notice has been taken.
(f) Judicial notice may be taken at any stage of the proceeding.
(g)
    (1) In a civil proceeding, the court shall instruct the jury to accept as conclusive any fact judicially noticed.
    (2) In a criminal proceeding, the court shall instruct the jury that it may, but is not required to, accept as conclusive any fact judicially noticed.

Article 2. Legislative Facts; Ordinances or Resolutions
§ 24-2-220. Judicial notice of legislative facts
The existence and territorial extent of states and their forms of government; all symbols of nationality; the laws of nations; all laws and resolutions of the General Assembly and the journals of each branch thereof as published by authority; the laws of the United States and of the several states thereof as published by authority; the uniform rules of the courts; the administrative rules and regulations filed with the Secretary of State pursuant to Code Section 50-13-6; the general customs of merchants; the admiralty and maritime courts of the world and their seals; the political makeup and history of this state and the federal government as well as the local divisions of this state; the seals of the several departments of the government of the United States and of the several states of the union; and all similar matters of legislative fact shall be judicially recognized without the introduction of proof. Judicial notice of adjudicative facts shall be governed by Code Section 24-2-201.

§ 24-2-221. Judicial notice of ordinance or resolution
When certified by a public officer, clerk, or keeper of county or municipal records in this state in a manner as specified for county records in Code Section 24-9-920 or in a manner as specified for municipal records in paragraph (1) or (2) of Code Section 24-9-902 and in the absence of contrary evidence, judicial notice may be taken of a certified copy of any ordinance or resolution included within a general codification required by paragraph (1) of subsection (b) of Code Section 36-80-19 as representing an ordinance or resolution duly approved by the governing authority and currently in force as presented. Any such certified copy shall be self-authenticating and shall be admissible as prima-facie proof of any such ordinance or resolution before any court or administrative body.

Chapter 3. Parol Evidence

§ 24-3-1. Parol evidence contradicting writing inadmissible generally
Parol contemporaneous evidence shall be generally inadmissible to contradict or vary the terms of a valid written instrument.

§ 24-3-2. Proof of unwritten portions of contract admissible where not inconsistent
If the writing does not purport to contain all the stipulations of the contract, parol evidence shall be admissible to prove other portions thereof not inconsistent with the writing; collateral undertakings between parties of the same part among themselves would not properly be looked for in the writing.

§ 24-3-3. Contemporaneous writings explaining each other; parol evidence explaining ambiguities
(a) All contemporaneous writings shall be admissible to explain each other.
(b) Parol evidence shall be admissible to explain all ambiguities, both latent and patent.

§ 24-3-4. Circumstances surrounding execution of contracts
The surrounding circumstances shall always be proper subjects of proof to aid in the construction of contracts.

§ 24-3-5. Known usage
Evidence of known and established usage shall be admissible to aid in the construction of contracts as well as to annex incidents.

§ 24-3-6. Rebuttal of equity; discharge of contract; proof of subsequent agreement; change of time or place of performance
Parol evidence shall be admissible to rebut an equity, to discharge an entire contract, to prove a new and distinct subsequent agreement, to enlarge the time of performance, or to change the place of performance.

§ 24-3-7. Proof of mistake in deed or written contract
Parol evidence shall be admissible to prove a mistake in a deed or any other contract required by law to be in writing.

§ 24-3-8. Original or subsequent voidness of writing
Parol evidence shall be admissible to show that a writing either was originally void or subsequently became void.

§ 24-3-9. Explanation or denial of receipts
Receipts for money shall always be only prima-facie evidence of payment and may be denied or explained by parol.

§ 24-3-10. Explanation of blank endorsements
Blank endorsements of negotiable paper may always be explained between the parties themselves or those taking with notice of dishonor or of the actual facts of such endorsements.

Chapter 4. Relevant Evidence and Its Limits

§ 24-4-401. "Relevant evidence" defined
As used in this chapter, the term "relevant evidence" means evidence having any tendency to make the existence of any fact that is of consequence to the determination of the action more probable or less probable than it would be without the evidence.

§ 24-4-402. Relevant evidence generally admissible; irrelevant evidence not admissible
All relevant evidence shall be admissible, except as limited by constitutional requirements or as otherwise provided by law or by other rules, as prescribed pursuant to constitutional or statutory authority, applicable in the court in which the matter is pending. Evidence which is not relevant shall not be admissible.

§ 24-4-403. Exclusion of relevant evidence on the grounds of prejudice, confusion, or waste of time
Relevant evidence may be excluded if its probative value is substantially outweighed by the danger of unfair prejudice, confusion of the issues, or misleading the jury or by considerations of undue delay, waste of time, or needless presentation of cumulative evidence.

§ 24-4-404. Character evidence not admissible to prove conduct; exceptions; other crimes
(a) Evidence of a person's character or a trait of character shall not be admissible for the purpose of proving action in conformity therewith on a particular occasion, except for:
(1) Evidence of a pertinent trait of character offered by an accused or by the prosecution to rebut the same; or if evidence of a trait of character of the alleged victim of the crime is offered by an accused and admitted under paragraph (2) of this subsection, evidence of the same trait of character of the accused offered by the prosecution;
(2) Subject to the limitations imposed by Code Section 24-4-412, evidence of a pertinent trait of character of the alleged victim of the crime offered by an accused or by the prosecution to rebut the same; or evidence of a character trait of peacefulness of the alleged victim offered by the prosecution in a homicide case to rebut evidence that the alleged victim was the first aggressor; or
(3) Evidence of the character of a witness, as provided in Code Sections 24-6-607, 24-6-608, and 24-6-609.
(b) Evidence of other crimes, wrongs, or acts shall not be admissible to prove the character of a person in order to show action in conformity therewith. It may, however, be admissible for other purposes, including, but not limited to, proof of motive, opportunity, intent, preparation, plan, knowledge, identity, or absence of mistake or accident. The prosecution in a criminal proceeding shall provide reasonable notice to the defense in advance of trial, unless pretrial notice is excused by the court upon good cause shown, of the general nature of any such evidence it intends to introduce at trial. Notice shall not be required when the evidence of prior crimes, wrongs, or acts is offered to prove the circumstances immediately surrounding the charged crime, motive, or prior difficulties between the accused and the alleged victim.

§ 24-4-405. Methods of proving character

(a) In all proceedings in which evidence of character or a trait of character of a person is admissible, proof shall be made by testimony as to reputation or by testimony in the form of an opinion.

(b) In proceedings in which character or a trait of character of a person is an essential element of a charge, claim, or defense or when an accused testifies to his or her own character, proof may also be made of specific instances of that person's conduct. The character of the accused, including specific instances of the accused's conduct, shall also be admissible in a presentencing hearing subject to the provisions of Code Section 17-10-2.

(c) On cross-examination, inquiry shall be allowable into relevant specific instances of conduct.

§ 24-4-406. Habit; routine practice

Evidence of the habit of a person or of the routine practice of an organization, whether corroborated or not and regardless of the presence of eyewitnesses, is relevant to prove that the conduct of the person or organization on a particular occasion was in conformity with such habit or routine practice.

§ 24-4-407. Subsequent remedial measures

In civil proceedings, when, after an injury or harm, remedial measures are taken to make such injury or harm less likely to recur, evidence of the remedial measures shall not be admissible to prove negligence or culpable conduct but may be admissible to prove product liability under subsection (b) or (c) of Code Section 51-1-11. The provisions of this Code section shall not require the exclusion of evidence of remedial measures when offered for impeachment or for another purpose, including, but not limited to, proving ownership, control, or feasibility of precautionary measures, if controverted.

§ 24-4-408. Compromises and offers to compromise

(a) Except as provided in Code Section 9-11-68, evidence of:

    (1) Furnishing, offering, or promising to furnish; or

    (2) Accepting, offering, or promising to accept

    a valuable consideration in compromising or attempting to compromise a claim which was disputed as to either validity or amount shall not be admissible to prove liability for or invalidity of any claim or its amount.

(b) Evidence of conduct or statements made in compromise negotiations or mediation shall not be admissible.

(c) This Code section shall not require the exclusion of any evidence otherwise discoverable merely because it is presented in the course of compromise negotiations or mediation. This Code section shall not require exclusion of evidence offered for another purpose, including, but not limited to, proving bias or prejudice of a witness, negating a contention of undue delay or abuse of process, or proving an effort to obstruct a criminal investigation or prosecution.

§ 24-4-409. Payment of medical and similar expenses
Evidence of furnishing, offering, or promising to pay medical, hospital, or similar expenses occasioned by an injury shall not be admissible to prove liability for the injury.

§ 24-4-410. Inadmissibility of pleas, plea discussions, and related statements
Except as otherwise provided by law, evidence of the following shall not, in any judicial or administrative proceeding, be admissible against the criminal defendant who made the plea or was a participant in the plea discussions:

(1) A plea of guilty which was later withdrawn;

(2) A plea of nolo contendere;

(3) Any statement made in the course of any proceedings in which a guilty plea or a plea of nolo contendere was entered and was later withdrawn, vacated, or set aside; or

(4) Any statement made in the course of plea discussions with an attorney for the prosecuting authority which does not result in a plea of guilty or which results in a plea of guilty later withdrawn, vacated, or set aside;

provided, however, that the statements described in paragraphs (1) through (4) of this Code section shall be admissible in any proceeding wherein another statement made in the course of the same plea or plea discussions has been introduced and the statement ought in fairness be considered contemporaneously with it or in a criminal proceeding for perjury or false statement if the statement was made by the accused under oath, on the record, and in the presence of counsel or after the accused voluntarily waived his or her right to counsel.

§ 24-4-411. Liability insurance
In all civil proceedings involving a claim for damages, evidence that a person was or was not insured against liability shall not be admissible except as provided in this Code section. This Code section shall not require the exclusion of evidence of insurance against liability in proceedings under Code Section 40-1-112 or when such evidence is offered for a relevant purpose, including, but not limited to, proof of agency, ownership, or control, and the court finds that the danger of unfair prejudice is substantially outweighed by the probative value of the evidence.

§ 24-4-412. Complainant's past sexual behavior not admissible in prosecutions for certain sexual offenses; exceptions

(a) In any prosecution for rape in violation of Code Section 16-6-1; aggravated assault with the intent to rape in violation of Code Section 16-5-21; trafficking persons for labor servitude or sexual servitude in violation of Code Section 16-5-46; aggravated sodomy or sodomy in violation of Code Section 16-6-2; statutory rape in violation of Code Section 16-6-3; aggravated child molestation or child molestation in violation of Code Section 16-6-4; keeping a place of prostitution in violation of Code Section 16-6-10; pimping in violation of Code Section 16-6-11; pandering in violation of Code Section 16-6-12; incest in violation of Code Section 16-6-22; sexual battery in violation of Code Section 16-6-22.1; or aggravated sexual battery in violation of Code Section 16-6-22.2, evidence relating to the past sexual behavior of the complaining witness shall not be admissible, either as direct evidence or on cross-examination of the complaining witness or other witnesses, except as provided in this Code section. For the purposes of this Code section, evidence of past sexual behavior includes, but is not limited to, evidence of the complaining witness's marital history, mode of dress, general reputation for promiscuity, nonchastity, or sexual mores contrary to the community standards.

(b) In any prosecution for rape in violation of Code Section 16-6-1; aggravated assault with the intent to rape in violation of Code Section 16-5-21; trafficking persons for labor servitude or sexual servitude in violation of Code Section 16-5-46; aggravated sodomy or sodomy in violation of Code Section 16-6-2; statutory rape in violation of Code Section 16-6-3; aggravated child molestation or child molestation in violation of Code Section 16-6-4; keeping a place of prostitution in violation of Code Section 16-6-10; pimping in violation of Code Section 16-6-11; pandering in violation of Code Section 16-6-12; incest in violation of Code Section 16-6-22; sexual battery in violation of Code Section 16-6-22.1; or aggravated sexual battery in violation of Code Section 16-6-22.2, the court may admit the following evidence relating to the past sexual behavior of the complaining witness, following the procedure described in subsection (c) of this Code section:

    (1) Evidence of specific instances of a victim's or complaining witness's sexual behavior, if offered to prove that someone other than the defendant was the source of semen, injury, or other physical evidence;

    (2) Evidence of specific instances of a victim's or complaining witness's sexual behavior with respect to the defendant if it supports an inference that the accused could have reasonably believed that the complaining witness consented to the conduct complained of in the prosecution;

    (3) Evidence of specific instances of a victim's or complaining witness's sexual behavior with respect to the defendant or another person if offered by the prosecutor; and

    (4) Evidence whose exclusion would violate the defendant's constitutional rights.

(c) The procedure for introducing evidence as described in subsection (b) of this Code section shall be as follows:

    (1) If a party intends to offer evidence under subsection (b) of this Code section, the party must:

        (A) File a motion that specifically describes the evidence and states the purpose for which it is to be offered; and

        (B) Do so at least three days before trial unless the court, for good cause, sets a different date; and

    (2) Before admitting the evidence under this Code section, the court shall conduct an in camera hearing to examine the merits of the motion.

§ 24-4-413. Evidence of similar transaction crimes in sexual assault cases

(a) In a criminal proceeding in which the accused is accused of an offense of sexual assault, evidence of the accused's commission of another offense of sexual assault shall be admissible and may be considered for its bearing on any matter to which it is relevant.

(b) In a proceeding in which the prosecution intends to offer evidence under this Code section, the prosecutor shall disclose such evidence to the accused, including statements of witnesses or a summary of the substance of any testimony that is expected to be offered, at least ten days in advance of trial, unless the time is shortened or lengthened or pretrial notice is excused by the judge upon good cause shown.

(c) This Code section shall not be the exclusive means to admit or consider evidence described in this Code section.

(d) As used in this Code section, the term "offense of sexual assault" means any conduct or attempt or conspiracy to engage in:

    (1) Conduct that would be a violation of Code Section 16-6-1, 16-6-2, 16-6-3, 16-6-5.1, 16-6-22, 16-6-22.1, or 16-6-22.2;

    (2) Any crime that involves contact, without consent, between any part of the accused's body or an object and the genitals or anus of another person;

    (3) Any crime that involves contact, without consent, between the genitals or anus of the accused and any part of another person's body; or

    (4) Any crime that involves deriving sexual pleasure or gratification from the infliction of death, bodily injury, or physical pain on another person.

§ 24-4-414. Evidence of similar transaction crimes in child molestation cases

(a) In a criminal proceeding in which the accused is accused of an offense of child molestation, evidence of the accused's commission of another offense of child molestation shall be admissible and may be considered for its bearing on any matter to which it is relevant.

(b) In a proceeding in which the state intends to offer evidence under this Code section, the prosecuting attorney shall disclose the evidence to the accused, including statements of witnesses or a summary of the substance of any testimony that the prosecuting attorney expects to offer, at least ten days in advance of trial, unless the time is shortened or lengthened or pretrial notice is excused by the judge upon good cause shown.

(c) This Code section shall not be the exclusive means to admit or consider evidence described under this Code section.

(d) As used in this Code section, the term "offense of child molestation" means any conduct or attempt or conspiracy to engage in:

    (1) Conduct that would be a violation of Code Section 16-6-4, 16-6-5, 16-12-100, 16-12-100.2, or 16-12-100.3;

    (2) Any crime that involves contact between any part of the accused's body or an object and the genitals or anus of a child;

    (3) Any crime that involves contact between the genitals or anus of the accused and any part of the body of a child; or

    (4) Any crime that involves deriving sexual pleasure or gratification from the infliction of death, bodily injury, or physical pain on a child.

§ 24-4-415. Evidence of similar acts in civil or administrative proceedings concerning sexual assault or child molestation

(a) In a civil or administrative proceeding in which a claim for damages or other relief is predicated on a party's alleged commission of conduct constituting an offense of sexual assault or an offense of child molestation, evidence of that party's commission of another offense of sexual assault or another offense of child molestation shall be admissible and may be considered as provided in Code Sections 24-4-413 and 24-4-414.

(b) A party who intends to offer evidence under this Code section shall disclose the evidence to the party against whom it will be offered, including statements of witnesses or a summary of the substance of any testimony that is expected to be offered, at least ten days in advance of trial, unless the time is shortened or lengthened or pretrial notice is excused by the judge upon good cause shown.

(c) This Code section shall not be the exclusive means to admit or consider evidence described in this Code section.

(d) As used in this Code section, the term:

  (1) "Offense of child molestation" means any conduct or attempt or conspiracy to engage in:

  (A) Conduct that would be a violation of Code Section 16-6-4, 16-6-5, 16-12-100, 16-12-100.2, or 16-12-100.3;

  (B) Any crime that involves contact between any part of the accused's body or an object and the genitals or anus of a child;

  (C) Any crime that involves contact between the genitals or anus of the accused and any part of the body of a child; or

  (D) Any crime that involves deriving sexual pleasure or gratification from the infliction of death, bodily injury, or physical pain on a child.

  (2) "Offense of sexual assault" means any conduct or attempt or conspiracy to engage in:

  (A) Conduct that would be a violation of Code Section 16-6-1, 16-6-2, 16-6-3, 16-6-5.1, 16-6-22, 16-6-22.1, or 16-6-22.2;

  (B) Any crime that involves contact, without consent, between any part of the accused's body or an object and the genitals or anus of another person;

  (C) Any crime that involves contact, without consent, between the genitals or anus of the accused and any part of another person's body; or

  (D) Any crime that involves deriving sexual pleasure or gratification from the infliction of death, bodily injury, or physical pain on another person.

§ 24-4-416. Statements of sympathy in medical malpractice cases

(a) As used in this Code section, the term "health care provider" means any person licensed under Chapter 9, 10A, 11, 11A, 26, 28, 30, 33, 34, 35, 39, or 44 of Title 43 or any hospital, nursing home, home health agency, institution, or medical facility licensed or defined under Chapter 7 of Title 31. The term shall also include any corporation, professional corporation, partnership, limited liability company, limited liability partnership, authority, or other entity composed of such health care providers.

(b) In any claim or civil proceeding brought by or on behalf of a patient allegedly experiencing an unanticipated outcome of medical care, any and all statements, affirmations, gestures, activities, or conduct expressing regret, apology, sympathy, commiseration, condolence, compassion, mistake, error, or a general sense of benevolence which is made by a health care provider or an employee or agent of a health care provider to the patient, a relative of the patient, or a representative of the patient and which relates to the unanticipated outcome shall be inadmissible as evidence and shall not constitute an admission of liability or an admission against interest.

§ 24-4-417. Evidence of similar acts in prosecutions for violations of Code Section 40-6-391

(a) In a criminal proceeding involving a prosecution for a violation of Code Section 40-6-391, evidence of the commission of another violation of Code Section 40-6-391 on a different occasion by the same accused shall be admissible when:

> **(1)** The accused refused in the current case to take the state administered test required by Code Section 40-5-55 and such evidence is relevant to prove knowledge, plan, or absence of mistake or accident;
>
> **(2)** The accused refused in the current case to provide an adequate breath sample for the state administered test required by Code Section 40-5-55 and such evidence is relevant to prove knowledge, plan, or absence of mistake or accident; or
>
> **(3)** The identity of the driver is in dispute in the current case and such evidence is relevant to prove identity.

(b) In a criminal proceeding in which the state intends to offer evidence under this Code section, the prosecuting attorney shall disclose such evidence to the accused, including statements of witnesses or a summary of the substance of any testimony that the prosecuting attorney expects to offer, at least ten days in advance of trial, unless the time is shortened or pretrial notice is excused by the judge upon good cause shown.

(c) This Code section shall not be the exclusive means to admit or consider evidence described in this Code section.

§ 24-4-418. Admissibility of criminal gang activity, disclosure

(a) In a criminal proceeding in which the accused is accused of conducting or participating in criminal gang activity in violation of Code Section 16-15-4, evidence of the accused's commission of criminal gang activity, as such term is defined in Code Section 16-15-3, shall be admissible and may be considered for its bearing on any matter to which it is relevant.

(b) In a proceeding in which the prosecution intends to offer evidence under this Code section, the prosecutor shall disclose such evidence to the accused, including statements of witnesses or a summary of the substance of any testimony that is expected to be offered, at least ten days in advance of trial, unless the time is shortened or lengthened or pretrial notice is excused by the judge upon good cause shown.

(c) This Code section shall not be the exclusive means to admit or consider evidence described in this Code section.

§ 24-4-419. Admission of criminal history record information

(a) As used in this Code section, the term "criminal history record information" shall have the same meaning as set forth in Code Section 35-3-30.

(b) In a civil proceeding against an employer, its employees, or its agents based on the conduct of an employee or former employee, criminal history record information shall not be admissible if:

   (1) The nature of such criminal history record information is not relevant to the facts underlying such proceeding or the veracity of the witness;

   (2) Prior to the act giving rise to such proceedings, criminal history record information was restricted or sealed as provided in Code Section 35-3-37, or a pardon for such conduct was granted; or

   (3) Such criminal history information is for an arrest or charge that did not result in a conviction.

Chapter 5. Privileges

§ 24-5-501. Certain communications privileged

(a) There are certain admissions and communications excluded from evidence on grounds of public policy, including, but not limited to, the following:
(1) Communications between husband and wife;
 (2) Communications between attorney and client;
 (3) Communications among grand jurors;
 (4) Secrets of state;
 (5) Communications between psychiatrist and patient;
 (6) Communications between licensed psychologist and patient as provided in Code Section 43-39-16;
 (7) Communications between a licensed clinical social worker, clinical nurse specialist in psychiatric/mental health, licensed marriage and family therapist, or licensed professional counselor and patient;
 (8) Communications between or among any psychiatrist, psychologist, licensed clinical social worker, clinical nurse specialist in psychiatric/mental health, licensed marriage and family therapist, and licensed professional counselor who are rendering psychotherapy or have rendered psychotherapy to a patient, regarding that patient's communications which are otherwise privileged by paragraph (5), (6), or (7) of this subsection; and
 (9) Communications between accountant and client as provided by Code Section 43-3-29.
(b) As used in this Code section, the term:
 (1) "Psychotherapy" means the employment of psychotherapeutic techniques.
 (2) "Psychotherapeutic techniques" shall have the same meaning as provided in Code Section 43-10A-3.

§ 24-5-502. Communications to clergyman privileged

Every communication made by any person professing religious faith, seeking spiritual comfort, or seeking counseling to any Protestant minister of the Gospel, any priest of the Roman Catholic faith, any priest of the Greek Orthodox Catholic faith, any Jewish rabbi, or any Christian or Jewish minister or similar functionary, by whatever name called, shall be deemed privileged. No such minister, priest, rabbi, or similar functionary shall disclose any communications made to him or her by any such person professing religious faith, seeking spiritual guidance, or seeking counseling, nor shall such minister, priest, rabbi, or similar functionary be competent or compellable to testify with reference to any such communication in any court.

§ 24-5-503. Husband and wife as witnesses for and against each other in criminal proceedings

(a) A husband and wife shall be competent but shall not be compellable to give evidence in any criminal proceeding for or against each other.

(b) The privilege created by subsection (a) of this Code section or by corresponding privileges in paragraph (1) of subsection (a) of Code Section 24-5-501 or subsection (a) of Code Section 24-5-505 shall not apply in proceedings in which:

(1) The husband or wife is charged with a crime against the person of a child under the age of 18, but such husband or wife shall be compellable to give evidence only on the specific act for which the accused is charged;

(2) The husband or wife is charged with a crime against his or her spouse;

(3) The husband or wife is charged with causing physical damage to property belonging to the husband and wife or to their separate property; or

(4) The alleged crime against his or her current spouse occurred prior to the lawful marriage of the husband and wife.

§ 24-5-504. Law enforcement officers testifying; home address

Any law enforcement officer testifying in his or her official capacity in any criminal proceeding shall not be compelled to reveal his or her home address. Such officer may be required to divulge the business address of his or her employer, and the court may require any law enforcement officer to answer questions as to his or her home address whenever such fact may be material to any issue in the proceeding.

§ 24-5-505. Party or witness privilege

(a) No party or witness shall be required to testify as to any matter which may incriminate or tend to incriminate such party or witness or which shall tend to bring infamy, disgrace, or public contempt upon such party or witness or any member of such party or witness's family.

(b) Except in proceedings in which a judgment creditor or judgment creditor's successor in interest seeks postjudgment discovery involving a judgment debtor pursuant to Code Section 9-11-69, no party or witness shall be required to testify as to any matter which shall tend to work a forfeiture of his or her estate.

(c) No official persons shall be called on to disclose any state matters of which the policy of the state and the interest of the community require concealment.

§ 24-5-506. Privilege against self-incrimination; testimony of accused in criminal case

(a) No person who is charged in any criminal proceeding with the commission of any criminal offense shall be compellable to give evidence for or against himself or herself.

(b) If an accused in a criminal proceeding wishes to testify and announces in open court his or her intention to do so, the accused may so testify. If an accused testifies, he or she shall be sworn as any other witness and, except as provided in Code Sections 24-6-608 and 24-6-609, may be examined and cross-examined as any other witness. The failure of an accused to testify shall create no presumption against the accused, and no comment shall be made because of such failure.

§ 24-5-507. Grant of immunity; contempt

(a) Whenever in the judgment of the Attorney General or any district attorney the testimony of any person or the production of evidence of any kind by any person in any criminal proceeding before a court or grand jury is necessary to the public interest, the Attorney General or the district attorney may request in writing the superior court to order such person to testify or produce the evidence. Upon order of the court, such person shall not be excused on the basis of the privilege against self-incrimination from testifying or producing any evidence required, but no testimony or other evidence required under the order or any information directly or indirectly derived from such testimony or evidence shall be used against the person in any proceeding or prosecution for a crime or offense concerning which he or she testified or produced evidence under court order. However, such person may nevertheless be prosecuted or subjected to penalty or forfeiture for any perjury, false swearing, or contempt committed in testifying or failing to testify or in producing or failing to produce evidence in accordance with the order but shall not be required to produce evidence that can be used in any other court of this state, the United States, or any other state. Any order entered under this Code section shall be entered of record in the minutes of the court so as to afford a permanent record thereof, and any testimony given by a person pursuant to such order shall be transcribed and filed for permanent record in the office of the clerk of the court.

(b) If a person refuses to testify after being granted immunity from prosecution and after being ordered to testify as set forth in this Code section, such person may be adjudged in contempt and committed to the county jail until such time as such person purges himself or herself of contempt by testifying as ordered without regard to the expiration of the grand jury. If the grand jury before which such person was ordered to testify has been dissolved, such person may purge himself or herself by testifying before the court.

§ 24-5-508. Qualified privilege for news gathering or dissemination

Any person, company, or other entity engaged in the gathering and dissemination of news for the public through any newspaper, book, magazine, radio or television broadcast, or electronic means shall have a qualified privilege against disclosure of any information, document, or item obtained or prepared in the gathering or dissemination of news in any proceeding where the one asserting the privilege is not a party, unless it is shown that this privilege has been waived or that what is sought:

    (1) Is material and relevant;

    (2) Cannot be reasonably obtained by alternative means; and

    (3) Is necessary to the proper preparation or presentation of the case of a party seeking the information, document, or item.

§ 24-5-509. Communications between victim of family violence or sexual assault and agents providing services to such victim; termination of privilege

§ 24-5-509. Communications between victim of family violence or sexual assault and agents providing services to such victim; termination of privilege

(a) As used in this Code section, the term:

(1) "Agent" means a current or former employee or volunteer of a program who has successfully completed a minimum of 20 hours of training in family violence and sexual assault intervention and prevention at a Criminal Justice Coordinating Council certified victim assistance program.

(2) "Family violence" shall have the same meaning as provided in Code Section 19-13-1.

(3) "Family violence shelter" means a program whose primary purpose is to provide services to family violence victims and their families that is not under the direct supervision of a law enforcement agency, prosecuting attorney's office, or a government agency.

(4) "Family violence victim" means a person who consults a family violence shelter for the purpose of securing advice or other services concerning an act of family violence, an alleged act of family violence, or an attempted act of family violence.

(5) "Government agency" means any agency of the executive, legislative, or judicial branch of government or political subdivision or authority thereof of this state, any other state, the District of Columbia, the United States and its territories and possessions, or any foreign government or international governmental or quasi-governmental agency recognized by the United States or by any of the several states.

(6) "Negative effect of the disclosure of the evidence on the victim" shall include the impact of the disclosure on the relationship between the victim and the agent and the delivery and accessibility of services.

(7) "Program" means a family violence shelter or rape crisis center.

(8) "Rape crisis center" means a program whose primary purpose is to provide services to sexual assault victims and their families that is not under the direct supervision of a law enforcement agency, prosecuting attorney's office, or a government agency.

(9) "Services" means any services provided to a victim by a program including but not limited to crisis hot lines, safe homes and shelters, assessment and intake, counseling, services for children who are victims of family violence or sexual assault, support in medical, administrative, and judicial systems, transportation, relocation, and crisis intervention. Such term shall not include mandatory reporting as required by Code Section 19-7-5 or 30-5-4.

(10) "Sexual assault" shall have the same meaning as provided in Code Section 17-5-70.

(11) "Sexual assault victim" means a person who consults a rape crisis center for the purpose of securing advice or other services concerning a sexual assault, an alleged sexual assault, or an attempted sexual assault.

(12) "Victim" means a family violence victim or sexual assault victim.

(b) No agent of a program shall be compelled to disclose any evidence in a judicial proceeding that the agent acquired while providing services to a victim, provided that such evidence was necessary to enable the agent to render services, unless the privilege has been waived by the victim or, upon motion by a party, the court finds by a preponderance of the evidence at a pretrial hearing or hearing outside the presence of the jury that:

§ 24-5-509. Communications between victim of family violence or sexual assault and agents providing services to such victim; termination of privilege

    (1) In a civil proceeding:
        (A) The evidence sought is material and relevant to factual issues to be determined;
        (B) The evidence is not sought solely for the purpose of referring to the victim's character for truthfulness or untruthfulness; provided, however, that this subparagraph shall not apply to evidence of the victim's prior inconsistent statements;
        (C) The evidence sought is not available or already obtained by the party seeking disclosure; and
        (D) The probative value of the evidence sought substantially outweighs the negative effect of the disclosure of the evidence on the victim; or
    (2) In a criminal proceeding:
        (A) The evidence sought is material and relevant to the issue of guilt, degree of guilt, or sentencing for the offense charged or a lesser included offense;
        (B) The evidence is not sought solely for the purpose of referring to the victim's character for truthfulness or untruthfulness; provided, however, that this subparagraph shall not apply to evidence of the victim's prior inconsistent statements;
        (C) The evidence sought is not available or already obtained by the party seeking disclosure; and
        (D) The probative value of the evidence sought substantially outweighs the negative effect of the disclosure of the evidence on the victim.

(c) If the court finds that the evidence sought may be subject to disclosure pursuant to subsection (b) of this Code section, the court shall order that such evidence be produced for the court under seal, shall examine the evidence in camera, and may allow disclosure of those portions of the evidence that the court finds are subject to disclosure under this Code section.

(d) The privilege afforded under this Code section shall terminate upon the death of the victim.

(e) The privilege granted by this Code section shall not apply if the agent was a witness or party to the family violence or sexual assault or other crime that occurred in the agent's presence.

(f) The mere presence of a third person during communications between an agent and a victim shall not void the privilege granted by this Code section, provided that the communication occurred in a setting when or where the victim had a reasonable expectation of privacy.

(g) If the victim is or has been judicially determined to be incompetent, the victim's guardian may waive the victim's privilege.

(h) In criminal proceedings, if either party intends to compel evidence based on this Code section, the party shall file and serve notice of his or her intention on the opposing party at least ten days prior to trial, or as otherwise directed by the court. The court shall hold a pretrial hearing in accordance with subsection (b) of this Code section and determine the issue prior to trial.

§ 24-5-510. Privileged communications between law enforcement officers and peer counselors

(a) As used in this Code section, the term:
   (1) "Client" means a public safety officer.
   (2) "Peer counselor" means:
      (A) An employee of the Office of Public Safety Support within the Department of Public Safety; or
      (B) An individual who is certified by the support coordinator of the Office of Public Safety Support within the Department of Public Safety pursuant to subsection (b) of Code Section 35-2-163 who is an employee of a public entity that employs public safety officers and who is designated by the executive head of such public entity.
   (3) "Public entity" shall have the same meaning as provided for in Code Section 35-2-160.
   (4) "Public safety officer" means a peace officer, correctional officer, emergency health worker, firefighter, highway emergency response operator, jail officer, juvenile correctional officer, probation officer, or emergency services dispatcher.

(b) Except as provided in subsection (c) of this Code section, communications between a client and a peer counselor shall be privileged. A peer counselor shall not disclose any such communications made to him or her and shall not be competent or compellable to testify with reference to any such communications in any court.

(c) The privilege created by subsection (b) of this Code section shall not apply when:
   (1) The disclosure is authorized by the client, or if the client is deceased, by his or her executor or administrator, and if an executor or administrator is not appointed, by the client's next of kin;
   (2) Compelled by court order;
   (3) The peer counselor was an initial responding public safety officer, witness, or party to an act that is the subject of the counseling;
   (4) The communication was made when the peer counselor was not performing official duties; or
   (5) The client is charged with a crime.

(d) The privilege created by this Code section shall not be grounds to fail to comply with mandatory reporting requirements as set forth in Code Section 19-7-5 or Chapter 5 of Title 30, the "Disabled Adults and Elder Persons Protection Act."

Chapter 6. Witnesses

Article 1. General Provisions

§ 24-6-601. General rule of competency
Except as otherwise provided in this chapter, every person is competent to be a witness.

§ 24-6-602. Lack of personal knowledge
A witness may not testify to a matter unless evidence is introduced sufficient to support a finding that the witness has personal knowledge of such matter. Evidence to prove personal knowledge may, but need not, consist of the witness's own testimony. The provisions of this Code section are subject to Code Section 24-7-703 and shall not apply to party admissions.

§ 24-6-603. Oath or affirmation
(a) Before testifying, every witness shall be required to declare that he or she will testify truthfully by oath or affirmation administered in a form calculated to awaken the witness's conscience and impress the witness's mind with the duty to do so.
(b) Notwithstanding the provisions of subsection (a) of this Code section, in all proceedings involving dependency as defined by Code Section 15-11-2 and in all criminal proceedings in which a child was a victim of or witness to any crime, the child shall be competent to testify, and the child's credibility shall be determined as provided in this chapter.

§ 24-6-604. Interpreters
Except as provided in Code Sections 24-6-656 and 24-6-657 or by the rules promulgated by the Supreme Court of Georgia pursuant to Code Section 15-1-14, an interpreter shall be subject to the provisions of Code Section 24-7-702. Interpreters shall be required to take an oath or affirmation to make a true translation.

§ 24-6-605. Judge as witness
The judge presiding at the trial shall not testify in that trial as a witness. No objection need be made in order to preserve this issue.

§ 24-6-606. Juror as witness
(a) A member of the jury shall not testify as a witness before that jury in the trial of the case in which the juror is sitting. If a juror is called to testify, the opposing party shall be afforded an opportunity to object out of the presence of the jury.
(b) Upon an inquiry into the validity of a verdict or indictment, a juror shall not testify by affidavit or otherwise nor shall a juror's statements be received in evidence as to any matter or statement occurring during the course of the jury's deliberations or to the effect of anything upon the jury deliberations or any other juror's mind or emotions as influencing the juror to assent to or dissent from the verdict or indictment or concerning the juror's mental processes in connection therewith; provided, however, that a juror may testify on the question of whether extraneous prejudicial information was improperly brought to the juror's attention, whether any outside influence was improperly brought to bear upon any juror, or whether there was a mistake in entering the verdict onto the verdict form.

§ 24-6-607. Who may impeach
The credibility of a witness may be attacked by any party, including the party calling the witness.

§ 24-6-608. Evidence of character and conduct of witness
(a) The credibility of a witness may be attacked or supported by evidence in the form of opinion or reputation, subject to the following limitations:

(1) The evidence may refer only to character for truthfulness or untruthfulness; and

(2) Evidence of truthful character shall be admissible only after the character of the witness for truthfulness has been attacked by opinion or reputation evidence or otherwise.

(b) Specific instances of the conduct of a witness, for the purpose of attacking or supporting the witness's character for truthfulness, other than a conviction of a crime as provided in Code Section 24-6-609, or conduct indicative of the witness's bias toward a party may not be proved by extrinsic evidence. Such instances may however, in the discretion of the court, if probative of truthfulness or untruthfulness, be inquired into on cross-examination of the witness:

(1) Concerning the witness's character for truthfulness or untruthfulness; or

(2) Concerning the character for truthfulness or untruthfulness of another witness as to which character the witness being cross-examined has testified.

(c) The giving of testimony, whether by an accused or by any other witness, shall not operate as a waiver of the accused's or the witness's privilege against self-incrimination when examined with respect to matters which relate only to character for truthfulness.

§ 24-6-609. Impeachment by evidence of conviction of a crime

(a) General rule. For the purpose of attacking the character for truthfulness of a witness:

(1) Evidence that a witness other than an accused has been convicted of a crime shall be admitted subject to the provisions of Code Section 24-4-403 if the crime was punishable by death or imprisonment in excess of one year under the law under which the witness was convicted and evidence that an accused has been convicted of such a crime shall be admitted if the court determines that the probative value of admitting the evidence outweighs its prejudicial effect to the accused; or

(2) Evidence that any witness has been convicted of a crime shall be admitted regardless of the punishment, if it readily can be determined that establishing the elements of such crime required proof or admission of an act of dishonesty or making a false statement.

(b) Time limit. Evidence of a conviction under this Code section shall not be admissible if a period of more than ten years has elapsed since the date of the conviction or of the release of the witness from the confinement imposed for such conviction, whichever is the later date, unless the court determines, in the interests of justice, that the probative value of the conviction supported by specific facts and circumstances substantially outweighs its prejudicial effect. However, evidence of a conviction more than ten years old, as calculated in this subsection, shall not be admissible unless the proponent gives to the adverse party sufficient advance written notice of intent to use such evidence to provide the adverse party with a fair opportunity to contest the use of such evidence.

(c) Effect of pardon, annulment, certificate of rehabilitation, or discharge from a first offender program. Evidence of a final adjudication of guilt and subsequent discharge under any first offender statute shall not be used to impeach any witness and evidence of a conviction shall not be admissible under this Code section if:

(1) The conviction has been the subject of a pardon, annulment, certificate of rehabilitation, or other equivalent procedure based on a finding of the rehabilitation of the person convicted, and that person has not been convicted of a subsequent crime which was punishable by death or imprisonment in excess of one year; or

(2) The conviction has been the subject of a pardon, annulment, or other equivalent procedure based on a finding of innocence.

(d) Nolo contendere pleas and juvenile adjudications. A conviction based on a plea of nolo contendere shall not be admissible to impeach any witness under this Code section. Evidence of juvenile adjudications shall not generally be admissible under this Code section. The court may, however, in a criminal proceeding allow evidence of a juvenile adjudication of a witness other than the accused if conviction of the offense would be admissible to attack the credibility of an adult and the court is satisfied that admission in evidence is necessary for a fair determination of the issue of guilt or innocence of the accused.

(e) Pendency of appeal. The pendency of an appeal shall not render evidence of a conviction inadmissible. Evidence of the pendency of an appeal shall be admissible.

§ 24-6-610. Religious beliefs or opinions
Evidence of the beliefs or opinions of a witness on matters of religion shall not be admissible for the purpose of proving that by reason of the nature of the beliefs or opinions the witness's credibility is impaired or enhanced.

§ 24-6-611. Mode and order of witness interrogation and presentation
(a) The court shall exercise reasonable control over the mode and order of interrogating witnesses and presenting evidence so as to:
   (1) Make the interrogation and presentation effective for the ascertainment of the truth;
   (2) Avoid needless consumption of time; and
   (3) Protect witnesses from harassment or undue embarrassment.
(b) A witness may be cross-examined on any matter relevant to any issue in the proceeding. The right of a thorough and sifting cross-examination shall belong to every party as to the witnesses called against the party. If several parties to the same proceeding have distinct interests, each party may exercise the right to cross-examination.
(c) Leading questions shall not be used on the direct examination of a witness except as may be necessary to develop the witness's testimony. Ordinarily leading questions shall be permitted on cross-examination. When a party calls a hostile witness, an adverse party, or a witness identified with an adverse party, interrogation may be by leading questions.

§ 24-6-612. Writing used to refresh memory
(a) If a witness uses a writing to refresh his or her memory while testifying, an adverse party shall be entitled to have the writing produced at the hearing or trial, to inspect it, to cross-examine the witness on such writing, and to introduce in evidence those portions of such writing which relate to the testimony of the witness.
(b) If a witness uses a writing to refresh his or her memory before testifying at trial and the court in its discretion determines it is necessary in the interests of justice, an adverse party shall be entitled to have the writing produced at the trial, to inspect it, to cross-examine the witness on such writing, and to introduce in evidence those portions of such writing which relate to the testimony of the witness. If the writing used is protected by the attorney-client privilege or as attorney work product under Code Section 9-11-26, use of the writing to refresh recollection prior to testifying shall not constitute a waiver of that privilege or protection. If it is claimed that the writing contains matters not related to the subject matter of the testimony, the court shall examine the writing in camera, excise any portions of such writing not so related, and order delivery of the remainder of such writing to the party entitled to such writing. Any portion withheld over objections shall be preserved and made available to the appellate court in the event of an appeal. If a writing is not produced or delivered pursuant to an order under this Code section, the court shall make any order justice requires; provided, however, that in criminal proceedings, when the prosecution elects not to comply, the order shall be one striking the testimony or, if the court in its discretion determines that the interests of justice so require, declaring a mistrial.

§ 24-6-613. Prior statements of witnesses

(a) In examining a witness concerning a prior statement made by the witness, whether written or not, the statement need not be shown nor its contents disclosed to the witness at that time; provided, however, upon request the same shall be shown or disclosed to opposing counsel.

(b) Except as provided in Code Section 24-8-806, extrinsic evidence of a prior inconsistent statement by a witness shall not be admissible unless the witness is first afforded an opportunity to explain or deny the prior inconsistent statement and the opposite party is afforded an opportunity to interrogate the witness on the prior inconsistent statement or the interests of justice otherwise require. This subsection shall not apply to admissions of a party-opponent as set forth in paragraph (2) of subsection (d) of Code Section 24-8-801.

(c) A prior consistent statement shall be admissible to rehabilitate a witness if the prior consistent statement logically rebuts an attack made on the witness's credibility. A general attack on a witness's credibility with evidence offered under Code Section 24-6-608 or 24-6-609 shall not permit rehabilitation under this subsection. If a prior consistent statement is offered to rebut an express or implied charge against the witness of recent fabrication or improper influence or motive, the prior consistent statement shall have been made before the alleged recent fabrication or improper influence or motive arose.

§ 24-6-614. Calling and interrogation of witnesses by court

(a) The court may, on its own motion, call a court appointed expert, call a witness regarding the competency of any party, or call a child witness or, at the suggestion of a party, call such witnesses, and all parties shall be entitled to cross-examine such witnesses. In all other situations, the court may only call witnesses when there is an agreement of all of the parties for the court to call such witnesses and all parties shall be entitled to cross-examine such witnesses.

(b) The court may interrogate witnesses whether called by itself pursuant to subsection (a) of this Code section or by a party.

(c) Objections to the calling of witnesses by the court or to interrogation by the court may be made at the time or at the next available opportunity when the jury is not present.

§ 24-6-615. Exclusion of witnesses

Except as otherwise provided in Code Section 24-6-616, at the request of a party the court shall order witnesses excluded so that each witness cannot hear the testimony of other witnesses, and it may make the order on its own motion. This Code section shall not authorize exclusion of:
    (1) A party who is a natural person;
    (2) An officer or employee of a party which is not a natural person designated as its representative by its attorney; or
    (3) A person whose presence is shown by a party to be essential to the presentation of the party's cause.

§ 24-6-616. Presence in courtroom of victim of criminal offense

Subject to the provisions of Code Section 17-17-9, the victim of a criminal offense shall be entitled to be present in any court exercising jurisdiction over such offense.

Article 2. Credibility

§ 24-6-620. Credibility a jury question

The credibility of a witness shall be a matter to be determined by the trier of fact, and if the case is being heard by a jury, the court shall give the jury proper instructions as to the credibility of a witness.

§ 24-6-621. Impeachment by contradiction

A witness may be impeached by disproving the facts testified to by the witness.

§ 24-6-622. Witness's feelings and relationship to parties provable

The state of a witness's feelings towards the parties and the witness's relationship to the parties may always be proved for the consideration of the jury.

§ 24-6-623. Treatment of witness

It shall be the right of a witness to be examined only as to relevant matters and to be protected from improper questions and from harsh or insulting demeanor.

Article 3. Use Of Sign Language and Intermediary Interpreter in Administrative and Judicial Proceedings

§ 24-6-650. State policy on hearing impaired persons

It is the policy of the State of Georgia to secure the rights of hearing impaired persons who, because of impaired hearing, cannot readily understand or communicate in spoken language and who consequently cannot equally participate in or benefit from proceedings, programs, and activities of the courts, legislative bodies, administrative agencies, licensing commissions, departments, and boards of this state and its political subdivisions unless qualified interpreters are available to assist such persons.

§ 24-6-651. Definitions

As used in this article, the term:

(1) "Agency" means any agency, authority, board, bureau, committee, commission, court, department, or jury of the legislative, judicial, or executive branch of government of this state or any political subdivision thereof.

(2) "Court qualified interpreter" means any person licensed as an interpreter for the hearing impaired pursuant to Code Section 15-1-14.

(3) "Hearing impaired person" means any person whose hearing is totally impaired or whose hearing is so seriously impaired as to prohibit the person from understanding oral communications when spoken in a normal conversational tone.

(4) "Intermediary interpreter" means any person, including any hearing impaired person, who is able to assist in providing an accurate interpretation between spoken English and sign language or between the variance of sign language by acting as an intermediary between a hearing impaired person and a qualified interpreter.

(5) "Proceeding" means any meeting, hearing, trial, investigation, or other proceeding of any nature conducted by an agency.

(6) "Qualified interpreter" means any person certified as an interpreter for hearing impaired persons by the Registry of Interpreters for the Deaf or a court qualified interpreter.

§ 24-6-652. Appointment of interpreters for hearing impaired persons interested in or witness at agency proceedings

(a) The agency conducting any proceeding shall provide a qualified interpreter to the hearing impaired person:

(1) Whenever the hearing impaired person is a party to the proceeding or a witness before the proceeding; or

(2) Whenever a person who is below the age of 18 years is a party to the proceeding or a witness before the proceeding conducted by an agency whose parents are hearing impaired persons or whose guardian is a hearing impaired person.

(b) A hearing impaired person shall notify the agency not less than ten days, excluding weekends and holidays, prior to the date of the proceeding of the need for a qualified interpreter. If the hearing impaired person received notice of the proceeding less than ten days, excluding weekends and holidays, prior to the proceeding, such person shall notify the agency as soon as practicable after receiving such notice.

§ 24-6-653. Procedure for interrogation and taking of statements from hearing impaired persons arrested for violation of criminal laws

(a) An arresting law enforcement agency shall provide a qualified interpreter to any hearing impaired person whenever a hearing impaired person is arrested for allegedly violating any criminal law or ordinance of this state or any political subdivision thereof.

(b)

(1) Except as provided in paragraph (2) of this subsection, no interrogation, warning, informing of rights, taking of statements, or other investigatory procedures shall be undertaken upon a hearing impaired person unless a qualified interpreter has been provided or the law enforcement agency has taken such other steps as may be reasonable to accommodate such person's disability. No answer, statement, admission, or other evidence acquired through the interrogation of a hearing impaired person shall be admissible in any criminal or quasi-criminal proceedings unless such was knowingly and voluntarily given. No hearing impaired person who has been taken into custody and who is otherwise eligible for release shall be detained because of the unavailability of a qualified interpreter.

(2) If a qualified interpreter is not available, an arresting officer may interrogate or take a statement from such person, provided that if the hearing impaired person cannot hear spoken words with a hearing aid or other sound amplification device, such interrogation and answers thereto shall be in writing and shall be preserved and turned over to the court in the event such person is tried for the alleged offense.

§ 24-6-654. Indigent hearing impaired defendants to be provided with interpreters

(a) A court shall provide a court qualified interpreter to any hearing impaired person whenever the hearing impaired person has been provided with a public defender or court appointed legal counsel.

(b) The court qualified interpreter authorized by this Code section shall be present at all times when the hearing impaired person is consulting with legal counsel.

D Judicial Proceedings

§ 24-6-655. Waiver of right to interpreter

Whenever a hearing impaired person shall be authorized to be provided a qualified interpreter, such person may waive the right to the use of such interpreter. Any such waiver shall be in writing and shall be approved by the agency or law enforcement agency before which the hearing impaired person is to appear. In no event shall the failure of a hearing impaired person to request an interpreter be deemed to be a waiver of the hearing impaired person's right to a qualified interpreter.

§ 24-6-656. Replacement of interpreters unable to communicate accurately with hearing impaired persons; appointment of intermediary interpreters

Whenever a hearing impaired person shall be authorized to be provided a qualified interpreter, the agency or law enforcement agency shall determine whether the qualified interpreter so provided is able to communicate accurately with and translate information to and from the hearing impaired person. If it is determined that the qualified interpreter cannot perform these functions, the agency or law enforcement agency shall obtain the services of another qualified interpreter or shall appoint an intermediary interpreter to assist the qualified interpreter in communicating with the hearing impaired person.

§ 24-6-657. Oath of interpreters; privileged communications; taping and filming of hearing impaired persons' testimony

(a) Prior to providing any service to a hearing impaired person, any qualified interpreter or intermediary interpreter shall subscribe to an oath that he or she will interpret all communications in an accurate manner to the best of his or her skill and knowledge. The Supreme Court of Georgia may by rule of court prescribe the form of the oath for interpreters and intermediary interpreters for use in court and other judicial proceedings.

(b) Whenever a hearing impaired person communicates with any other person through the use of an interpreter and under circumstances which make such communications privileged or otherwise confidential, the presence of the interpreter shall not vitiate such privilege and the interpreter shall not be required to disclose the contents of such communication.

(c) Whenever a qualified interpreter is required by this article, the agency or law enforcement agency shall not begin the proceeding or take any action until such interpreter is in full view of and spatially situated so as to assure effective communication with the hearing impaired person.

(d) The agency or law enforcement agency may, upon its own motion or upon motion of any party, witness, or participant, order that the testimony of the hearing impaired person be electronically and visually recorded. Any such recording may be used to verify the testimony given by the hearing impaired person.

§ 24-6-658. Compensation of interpreters

Any qualified interpreter or intermediary interpreter providing service under this article shall be compensated by the agency or law enforcement agency requesting such service.

Chapter 7. Opinions and Expert Testimony

§ 24-7-701. Lay witness opinion testimony

(a) If the witness is not testifying as an expert, the witness's testimony in the form of opinions or inferences shall be limited to those opinions or inferences which are:

    (1) Rationally based on the perception of the witness;

    (2) Helpful to a clear understanding of the witness's testimony or the determination of a fact in issue; and

    (3) Not based on scientific, technical, or other specialized knowledge within the scope of Code Section 24-7-702.

(b) Direct testimony as to market value is in the nature of opinion evidence. A witness need not be an expert or dealer in an article or property to testify as to its value if he or she has had an opportunity to form a reasoned opinion.

§ 24-7-702. Expert opinion testimony in civil actions; medical experts; pretrial hearings; precedential value of federal law

(a) Except as provided in Code Section 22-1-14 and in subsection (g) of this Code section, the provisions of this Code section shall apply in all proceedings. The opinion of a witness qualified as an expert under this Code section may be given on the facts as proved by other witnesses.

(b) A witness who is qualified as an expert by knowledge, skill, experience, training, or education may testify in the form of an opinion or otherwise, if:

    (1) The expert's scientific, technical, or other specialized knowledge will help the trier of fact to understand the evidence or to determine a fact in issue;

    (2) The testimony is based upon sufficient facts or data;

    (3) The testimony is the product of reliable principles and methods; and

    (4) The expert has reliably applied the principles and methods to the facts of the case.

(c) Notwithstanding the provisions of subsection (b) of this Code section and any other provision of law which might be construed to the contrary, in professional malpractice actions, the opinions of an expert, who is otherwise qualified as to the acceptable standard of conduct of the professional whose conduct is at issue, shall be admissible only if, at the time the act or omission is alleged to have occurred, such expert:

    (1) Was licensed by an appropriate regulatory agency to practice his or her profession in the state in which such expert was practicing or teaching in the profession at such time; and

    (2) In the case of a medical malpractice action, had actual professional knowledge and experience in the area of practice or specialty in which the opinion is to be given as the result of having been regularly engaged in:

        (A) The active practice of such area of specialty of his or her profession for at least three of the last five years, with sufficient frequency to establish an appropriate level of knowledge, as determined by the judge, in performing the procedure, diagnosing the condition, or rendering the treatment which is alleged to have been performed or rendered negligently by the defendant whose conduct is at issue; or

§ 24-7-702. Expert opinion testimony in civil actions; medical experts; pretrial hearings; precedential value of federal law

    (B) The teaching of his or her profession for at least three of the last five years as an employed member of the faculty of an educational institution accredited in the teaching of such profession, with sufficient frequency to establish an appropriate level of knowledge, as determined by the judge, in teaching others how to perform the procedure, diagnose the condition, or render the treatment which is alleged to have been performed or rendered negligently by the defendant whose conduct is at issue; and
    (C) Except as provided in subparagraph (D) of this paragraph:
        (i) Is a member of the same profession;
        (ii) Is a medical doctor testifying as to the standard of care of a defendant who is a doctor of osteopathy; or
        (iii) Is a doctor of osteopathy testifying as to the standard of care of a defendant who is a medical doctor; and
    (D) Notwithstanding any other provision of this Code section, an expert who is a physician and, as a result of having, during at least three of the last five years immediately preceding the time the act or omission is alleged to have occurred, supervised, taught, or instructed nurses, nurse practitioners, certified registered nurse anesthetists, nurse midwives, physician assistants, physical therapists, occupational therapists, or medical support staff, has knowledge of the standard of care of that health care provider under the circumstances at issue shall be competent to testify as to the standard of that health care provider. However, a nurse, nurse practitioner, certified registered nurse anesthetist, nurse midwife, physician assistant, physical therapist, occupational therapist, or medical support staff shall not be competent to testify as to the standard of care of a physician.

(d) Upon motion of a party, the court may hold a pretrial hearing to determine whether the witness qualifies as an expert and whether the expert's testimony satisfies the requirements of subsections (a) and (b) of this Code section. In all civil proceedings, a hearing and any ruling shall be completed no later than the final pretrial conference contemplated under Code Section 9-11-16.

(e) In all civil proceedings, an affiant shall meet the requirements of this Code section in order to be deemed qualified to testify as an expert by means of the affidavit required under Code Section 9-11-9.1.

(f) It is the intent of the legislature that, in all proceedings, the courts of the State of Georgia not be viewed as open to expert evidence that would not be admissible in other states. Therefore, in interpreting and applying this Code section, the courts of this state may draw from the opinions of the United States Supreme Court in Daubert v. Merrell Dow Pharmaceuticals, Inc., 509 U.S. 579 (1993); General Electric Co. v. Joiner, 522 U.S. 136 (1997); Kumho Tire Co. Ltd. v. Carmichael, 526 U.S. 137 (1999); and other cases in federal courts applying the standards announced by the United States Supreme Court in these cases.

(g) This Code section shall not be strictly applied in proceedings conducted pursuant to Chapter 9 of Title 34 or in administrative proceedings conducted pursuant to Chapter 13 of Title 50.

§ 24-7-703. Bases of expert opinion testimony
The facts or data in the particular proceeding upon which an expert bases an opinion or inference may be those perceived by or made known to the expert at or before the hearing. If of a type reasonably relied upon by experts in the particular field in forming opinions or inferences upon the subject, such facts or data need not be admissible in evidence in order for the opinion or inference to be admitted. Such facts or data that are otherwise inadmissible shall not be disclosed to the jury by the proponent of the opinion or inference unless the court determines that their probative value in assisting the jury to evaluate the expert's opinion substantially outweighs their prejudicial effect.

§ 24-7-704. Ultimate issue opinion
(a) Except as provided in subsection (b) of this Code section, testimony in the form of an opinion or inference otherwise admissible shall not be objectionable because it embraces an ultimate issue to be decided by the trier of fact.
(b) No expert witness testifying with respect to the mental state or condition of an accused in a criminal proceeding shall state an opinion or inference as to whether the accused did or did not have the mental state or condition constituting an element of the crime charged or of a defense thereto. Such ultimate issues are matters for the trier of fact alone.

§ 24-7-705. Disclosure of facts or data underlying expert opinion
An expert may testify in terms of opinion or inference and give reasons therefor without first testifying to the underlying facts or data, unless the court requires otherwise. An expert may in any event be required to disclose the underlying facts or data on cross-examination.

§ 24-7-706. Court appointed experts

Except as provided in Chapter 7 of Title 9 or Code Section 17-7-130.1, 17-10-66, 29-4-11, 29-5-11, 31-14-3, 31-20-3, 44-6-166.1, 44-6-184, or 44-6-187, the following procedures shall govern the appointment, compensation, and presentation of testimony of court appointed experts:

   (1) The court on its own motion or on the motion of any party may enter an order to show cause why any expert witness should not be appointed and may request the parties to submit nominations. The court may appoint any expert witnesses agreed upon by the parties and may appoint expert witnesses of its own selection. An expert witness shall not be appointed by the court unless the witness consents to act. Each appointed expert witness shall be informed of his or her duties by the court in writing, a copy of which shall be filed with the clerk, or at a conference in which the parties shall have opportunity to participate. Each appointed expert witness shall advise the parties of his or her findings, if any. Except as provided in Article 3 of Chapter 12 or Article 6 of Chapter 13 of this title, such witness's deposition may be taken by any party. Such witness may be called to testify by the court or any party. Each expert witness shall be subject to cross-examination by each party, including a party calling the witness;

   (2) Appointed expert witnesses shall be entitled to reasonable compensation in whatever sum the court allows. The compensation fixed shall be payable from funds which may be provided by law in criminal proceedings and civil proceedings involving just compensation for the taking of property. In other civil proceedings, the compensation shall be paid by the parties in such proportion and at such time as the court directs and thereafter charged in like manner as other costs;

   (3) In the exercise of its discretion, the court may authorize disclosure to the jury of the fact that the court appointed the expert witness; and

   (4) Nothing in this Code section shall limit a party in calling expert witnesses of the party's own selection.

§ 24-7-707. Expert opinion testimony in criminal proceedings

In criminal proceedings, the opinions of experts on any question of science, skill, trade, or like questions shall always be admissible; and such opinions may be given on the facts as proved by other witnesses.

Chapter 8. Hearsay

Article 1. General Provisions

§ 24-8-801. Definitions

As used in this chapter, the term:

(a) "Statement" means:

(1) An oral or written assertion; or

(2) Nonverbal conduct of a person, if it is intended by the person as an assertion.

(b) "Declarant" means a person who makes a statement.

(c) "Hearsay" means a statement, other than one made by the declarant while testifying at the trial or hearing, offered in evidence to prove the truth of the matter asserted.

(d) "Hearsay" shall be subject to the following exclusions and conditions:

(1) Prior statement by witness.

(A) An out-of-court statement shall not be hearsay if the declarant testifies at the trial or hearing, is subject to cross-examination concerning the statement, and the statement is admissible as a prior inconsistent statement or a prior consistent statement under Code Section 24-6-613 or is otherwise admissible under this chapter.

(B) If a hearsay statement is admitted and the declarant does not testify at the trial or hearing, other out-of-court statements of the declarant shall be admissible for the limited use of impeaching or rehabilitating the credibility of the declarant, and not as substantive evidence, if the other statements qualify as prior inconsistent statements or prior consistent statements under Code Section 24-6-613.

(C) A statement shall not be hearsay if the declarant testifies at the trial or hearing and is subject to cross-examination concerning the statement, and the statement is one of identification of a person made after perceiving the person; and

(2) Admissions by party-opponent. Admissions shall not be excluded by the hearsay rule. An admission is a statement offered against a party which is:

(A) The party's own statement, in either an individual or representative capacity;

(B) A statement of which the party has manifested an adoption or belief in its truth;

(C) A statement by a person authorized by the party to make a statement concerning the subject;

(D) A statement by the party's agent or employee, but not including any agent of the state in a criminal proceeding, concerning a matter within the scope of the agency or employment, made during the existence of the relationship; or

(E) A statement by a coconspirator of a party during the course and in furtherance of the conspiracy, including a statement made during the concealment phase of a conspiracy. A conspiracy need not be charged in order to make a statement admissible under this subparagraph.

The contents of the statement shall be considered but shall not alone be sufficient to establish the declarant's authority under subparagraph (C) of this paragraph, the agency or employment relationship and scope thereof under subparagraph (D) of this paragraph, or the existence of the conspiracy and the participation therein of the declarant and the party against whom the statement is offered under subparagraph (E) of this paragraph.

(e) "Public office" means:

(1) Every state department, agency, board, bureau, commission, division, public corporation, and authority;

(2) Every county, municipal corporation, school district, or other political subdivision of this state;

(3) Every department, agency, board, bureau, commission, authority, or similar body of each such county, municipal corporation, or other political subdivision of this state; and

(4) Every city, county, regional, or other authority established pursuant to the laws of this state.

(f) "Public official" means an elected or appointed official.

(g) "Public record" means information that is inscribed on a tangible medium or that is stored in an electronic or other medium and is retrievable in perceivable form and created in the course of the operation of a public office.

§ 24-8-802. Hearsay rule

Hearsay shall not be admissible except as provided by this article; provided, however, that if a party does not properly object to hearsay, the objection shall be deemed waived, and the hearsay evidence shall be legal evidence and admissible.

§ 24-8-803. Hearsay rule exceptions; availability of declarant immaterial

The following shall not be excluded by the hearsay rule, even though the declarant is available as a witness:

(1) Present sense impression. A statement describing or explaining an event or condition made while the declarant was perceiving the event or condition or immediately thereafter;

(2) Excited utterance. A statement relating to a startling event or condition made while the declarant was under the stress of excitement caused by the event or condition;

(3) Then existing mental, emotional, or physical condition. A statement of the declarant's then existing state of mind, emotion, sensation, or physical condition, such as intent, plan, motive, design, mental feeling, pain, and bodily health, but not including a statement of memory or belief to prove the fact remembered or believed unless such statements relate to the execution, revocation, identification, or terms of the declarant's will and not including a statement of belief as to the intent of another person;

(4) Statements for purposes of medical diagnosis or treatment. Statements made for purposes of medical diagnosis or treatment and describing medical history, or past or present symptoms, pain, or sensations, or the inception or general character of the cause or external source thereof insofar as reasonably pertinent to diagnosis or treatment;

(5) Recorded recollection. A memorandum or record concerning a matter about which a witness once had knowledge but now has insufficient recollection to enable the witness to testify fully and accurately shown to have been made or adopted by the witness when the matter was fresh in the witness's memory and to reflect that knowledge correctly. If admitted, the memorandum or record may be read into evidence but shall not itself be received as an exhibit unless offered by an adverse party;

(6) Records of regularly conducted activity. Unless the source of information or the method or circumstances of preparation indicate lack of trustworthiness and subject to the provisions of Chapter 7 of this title, a memorandum, report, record, or data compilation, in any form, of acts, events, conditions, opinions, or diagnoses, if

    (A) made at or near the time of the described acts, events, conditions, opinions, or diagnoses;
    (B) made by, or from information transmitted by, a person with personal knowledge and a business duty to report;
    (C) kept in the course of a regularly conducted business activity; and
    (D) it was the regular practice of that business activity to make the memorandum, report, record, or data compilation,

all as shown by the testimony of the custodian or other qualified witness or by certification that complies with paragraph (11) or (12) of Code Section 24-9-902 or by any other statute permitting certification. The term "business" as used in this paragraph includes any business, institution, association, profession, occupation, and calling of every kind, whether or not conducted for profit. Public records and reports shall be admissible under paragraph (8) of this Code section and shall not be admissible under this paragraph;

(7) Absence of entry in records kept in accordance with paragraph (6) of this Code section. Evidence that a matter is not included in the memoranda, reports, records, or data compilations, in any form, kept in accordance with the provisions of paragraph (6) of this Code section, to prove the nonoccurrence or nonexistence of the matter, if the matter was of a kind of which a memorandum, report, record, or data compilation was regularly made and preserved, unless the sources of information or other circumstances indicate lack of trustworthiness;

(8) Public records and reports. Except as otherwise provided by law, public records, reports, statements, or data compilations, in any form, of public offices, setting forth:

    (A) The activities of the public office;
    (B) Matters observed pursuant to duty imposed by law as to which matters there was a duty to report, excluding, however, against the accused in criminal proceedings, matters observed by police officers and other law enforcement personnel in connection with an investigation; or
    (C) In civil proceedings and against the state in criminal proceedings, factual findings resulting from an investigation made pursuant to authority granted by law, unless the sources of information or other circumstances indicate lack of trustworthiness;

§ 24-8-803. Hearsay rule exceptions; (9) Records of vital statistics

(9) Records of vital statistics. Records or data compilations, in any form, of births, fetal deaths, deaths, or marriages, if the report thereof was made to a public office pursuant to requirements of law;

(10) Absence of public record or entry. To prove the absence of a record, report, statement, or data compilation, in any form, or the nonoccurrence or nonexistence of a matter of which a record, report, statement, or data compilation, in any form, was regularly made and preserved by a public office, evidence in the form of a certification in accordance with Code Section 24-9-902, or testimony, that diligent search failed to disclose the record, report, statement, or data compilation, or entry;

(11) Records of religious organizations. Statements of birth, marriages, divorces, deaths, legitimacy, ancestry, relationship by blood or marriage, or other similar facts of personal or family history, contained in a regularly kept record of a religious organization;

(12) Marriage, baptismal, and similar certificates. Statements of fact contained in a certificate that the maker performed a marriage or other ceremony or administered a sacrament, made by a clergyman, public official, or other person authorized by the rules or practices of a religious organization or by law to perform the act certified and purporting to have been issued at the time of the act or within a reasonable time thereafter;

(13) Family records. Statements of fact concerning personal or family history contained in family Bibles, genealogies, charts, engravings on rings, inscriptions on family portraits, engravings on urns, crypts, or tombstones, or the like;

(14) Records of documents affecting an interest in property. The record of a document purporting to establish or affect an interest in property, as proof of the content of the original recorded document and its execution and delivery by each person by whom it purports to have been executed, if the record is a record of a public office and an applicable law authorizes the recording of documents of that kind in such office;

(15) Statements in documents affecting an interest in property. A statement contained in a document purporting to establish or affect an interest in property if the matter stated was relevant to the purpose of the document, unless dealings with the property since the document was made have been inconsistent with the truth of the statement or the purport of the document;

(16) Statements in ancient documents. Statements in a document in existence 20 years or more the authenticity of which is established;

(17) Market reports and commercial publications. Market quotations, tabulations, lists, directories, or other published compilations generally used and relied upon by the public or by persons in the witness's particular occupation;

(18) Learned treatises. To the extent called to the attention of an expert witness upon cross-examination, statements contained in published treatises, periodicals, or pamphlets, whether published electronically or in print, on a subject of history, medicine, or other science or art, established as a reliable authority by the testimony or admission of the witness, by other expert testimony, or by judicial notice. If admitted, the statements may be used for cross-examination of an expert witness and read into evidence but shall not be received as exhibits;

§ 24-8-803. Hearsay rule exceptions;
(19) Reputation concerning personal or family history.

(19) Reputation concerning personal or family history. Reputation among members of a person's family by blood, adoption, or marriage or among a person's associates or in the community concerning a person's birth, adoption, marriage, divorce, death, legitimacy, relationship by blood, adoption, or marriage, ancestry, or other similar fact of the person's personal or family history;

(20) Reputation concerning boundaries or general history. Reputation in a community, arising before the controversy, as to boundaries of or customs affecting lands in the community and reputation as to events of general history important to the community or state or nation in which such lands are located;

(21) Reputation as to character. Reputation of a person's character among associates or in the community;

(22) Judgment of previous conviction. Evidence of a final judgment, entered after a trial or upon a plea of guilty but not upon a plea of nolo contendere, adjudging a person guilty of a crime punishable by death or imprisonment in excess of one year to prove any fact essential to sustain the judgment, but not including, when offered by the state in a criminal prosecution for purposes other than impeachment, judgments against persons other than the accused. The pendency of an appeal may be shown but shall not affect admissibility; or

(23) Judgment as to personal, family, or general history or boundaries. Judgments as proof of matters of personal, family, or general history or boundaries essential to the judgment, if the same would be provable by evidence of reputation.

§ 24-8-804. Hearsay rule exceptions; declarant unavailable

(a) As used in this Code section, the term "unavailable as a witness" includes situations in which the declarant:

   (1) Is exempted by ruling of the court on the ground of privilege from testifying concerning the subject matter of the declarant's statement;

   (2) Persists in refusing to testify concerning the subject matter of the declarant's statement despite an order of the court to do so;

   (3) Testifies to a lack of memory of the subject matter of the declarant's statement;

   (4) Is unable to be present or to testify at the hearing because of death or then existing physical or mental illness or infirmity; or

   (5) Is absent from the hearing and the proponent of the statement has been unable to procure the declarant's attendance or, in the case of exceptions under paragraph (2), (3), or (4) of subsection (b) of this Code section, the declarant's attendance or testimony, by process or other reasonable means.

A declarant shall not be deemed unavailable as a witness if the declarant's exemption, refusal, claim of lack of memory, inability, or absence is due to the procurement or wrongdoing of the proponent of a statement for the purpose of preventing the witness from attending or testifying.

§ 24-8-804(b). Hearsay rule exceptions

(b) The following shall not be excluded by the hearsay rule if the declarant is unavailable as a witness:

(1) Testimony given as a witness at another hearing of the same or a different proceeding, or in a deposition taken in compliance with law in the course of the same or another proceeding, if the party against whom the testimony is now offered, or, in a civil proceeding, a predecessor in interest, had an opportunity and similar motive to develop the testimony by direct, cross, or redirect examination. If deposition testimony is admissible under either the rules stated in Code Section 9-11-32 or this Code section, it shall be admissible at trial in accordance with the rules under which it was offered;

(2) In a prosecution for homicide or in a civil proceeding, a statement made by a declarant while believing that his or her death was imminent, concerning the cause or circumstances of what the declarant believed to be impending death;

(3) A statement against interest. A statement against interest is a statement:

(A) Which a reasonable person in the declarant's position would have made only if the person believed it to be true because, when made, it was so contrary to the declarant's proprietary or pecuniary interest or had so great a tendency to invalidate a claim by the declarant against another or to expose the declarant to civil or criminal liability; and

(B) Supported by corroborating circumstances that clearly indicate the trustworthiness of the statement if it is offered in a criminal case as a statement that tends to expose the declarant to criminal liability;

(4) A statement concerning the declarant's own birth, adoption, marriage, divorce, legitimacy, relationship by blood, adoption, or marriage, ancestry, or other similar fact of personal or family history, even though the declarant had no means of acquiring personal knowledge of the matter stated or a statement concerning the foregoing matters and death also of another person, if the declarant was related to the other by blood, adoption, or marriage or was so intimately associated with the other's family as to be likely to have accurate information concerning the matter declared; or

(5) A statement offered against a party that has engaged or acquiesced in wrongdoing that was intended to, and did, procure the unavailability of the declarant as a witness.

§ 24-8-805. Hearsay within hearsay
Hearsay included within hearsay shall not be excluded under the hearsay rule if each part of the combined statements conforms with an exception to the hearsay rule.

§ 24-8-806. Attacking and supporting credibility of a declarant
When a hearsay statement has been admitted in evidence, the credibility of the declarant may be attacked and, if attacked, may be supported by any evidence which would be admissible for those purposes if the declarant had testified as a witness. Evidence of a statement or conduct by the declarant at any time, inconsistent with the declarant's hearsay statement, shall not be subject to any requirement that the declarant may have been afforded an opportunity to deny or explain. If the party against whom a hearsay statement has been admitted calls the declarant as a witness, the party shall be entitled to examine the declarant on the statement as if under cross-examination.

§ 24-8-807. Residual exception
A statement not specifically covered by any law but having equivalent circumstantial guarantees of trustworthiness shall not be excluded by the hearsay rule, if the court determines that:
    (1) The statement is offered as evidence of a material fact;
    (2) The statement is more probative on the point for which it is offered than any other evidence which the proponent can procure through reasonable efforts; and
    (3) The general purposes of the rules of evidence and the interests of justice will best be served by admission of the statement into evidence.

However, a statement may not be admitted under this Code section unless the proponent of it makes known to the adverse party, sufficiently in advance of the trial or hearing to provide the adverse party with a fair opportunity to prepare to meet it, the proponent's intention to offer the statement and the particulars of it, including the name and address of the declarant.

Article 2. Admissions and Confessions

§ 24-8-820. Testimony as to child's description of sexual contact or physical abuse
(a) A statement made by a child younger than 16 years of age describing any act of sexual contact or physical abuse performed with or on such child by another or with or on another in the presence of such child shall be admissible in evidence by the testimony of the person to whom made if the proponent of such statement provides notice to the adverse party prior to trial of the intention to use such out-of-court statement and such child testifies at the trial, unless the adverse party forfeits or waives such child's testimony as provided in this title, and, at the time of the testimony regarding the out-of-court statements, the person to whom the child made such statement is subject to cross-examination regarding the out-of-court statements.
(b) This Code section shall apply to any motion made or hearing or trial commenced on or after April 18, 2019.

§ 24-8-821. Admissions in pleadings
Without offering the same in evidence, either party may avail himself or herself of allegations or admissions made in the pleadings of the other.

§ 24-8-822. Right to have whole conversation heard
When an admission is given in evidence by one party, it shall be the right of the other party to have the whole admission and all the conversation connected therewith admitted into evidence.

§ 24-8-823. Admissions and confessions received with care; no conviction on uncorroborated confession
All admissions shall be scanned with care, and confessions of guilt shall be received with great caution. A confession alone, uncorroborated by any other evidence, shall not justify a conviction.

§ 24-8-824. Only voluntary confessions admissible
To make a confession admissible, it shall have been made voluntarily, without being induced by another by the slightest hope of benefit or remotest fear of injury.

§ 24-8-825. Confessions under spiritual exhortation, promise of secrecy, or collateral benefit admissible
The fact that a confession has been made under a spiritual exhortation, a promise of secrecy, or a promise of collateral benefit shall not exclude it.

§ 24-8-826. Medical reports in narrative form
(a) Upon the trial of any civil proceeding involving injury or disease, any medical report in narrative form which has been signed and dated by an examining or treating licensed physician, dentist, orthodontist, podiatrist, physical or occupational therapist, doctor of chiropractic, psychologist, advanced practice registered nurse, social worker, professional counselor, or marriage and family therapist shall be admissible and received in evidence insofar as it purports to represent the history, examination, diagnosis, treatment, prognosis, or interpretation of tests or examinations, including the basis therefor, by the person signing the report, the same as if that person were present at trial and testifying as a witness; provided, however, that such report and notice of intention to introduce such report shall first be provided to the adverse party at least 60 days prior to trial. A statement of the qualifications of the person signing such report may be included as part of the basis for providing the information contained therein, and the opinion of the person signing the report with regard to the etiology of the injury or disease may be included as part of the diagnosis. Any adverse party may object to the admissibility of any portion of the report, other than on the ground that it is hearsay, within 15 days of being provided with the report. Further, any adverse party shall have the right to cross-examine the person signing the report and provide rebuttal testimony. The party tendering the report may also introduce testimony of the person signing the report for the purpose of supplementing the report or otherwise.
(b) The medical narrative shall be presented to the jury as depositions are presented to the jury and shall not go out with the jury as documentary evidence.

Chapter 9. Authentication and Identification

Article 1. General Provisions

§ 24-9-901. Requirement of authentication or identification

(a) The requirement of authentication or identification as a condition precedent to admissibility shall be satisfied by evidence sufficient to support a finding that the matter in question is what its proponent claims.

(b) By way of illustration only, and not by way of limitation, the following are examples of authentication or identification conforming with the requirements of this Code section:

(1) Testimony of a witness with knowledge that a matter is what it is claimed to be;

(2) Nonexpert opinion as to the genuineness of handwriting, based upon familiarity not acquired for purposes of the litigation;

(3) Comparison by the trier of fact or by expert witnesses with specimens which have been authenticated. Such specimens shall be furnished to the opposite party no later than ten days prior to trial;

(4) Appearance, contents, substance, internal patterns, or other distinctive characteristics, taken in conjunction with circumstances;

(5) Identification of a voice, whether heard firsthand or through mechanical or electronic transmission or recording, by opinion based upon hearing the voice at any time under circumstances connecting it with the alleged speaker;

(6) Telephone conversations, by evidence that a call was made to the number assigned at the time by a telephone service provider to a particular person or business, if:

   (A) In the case of a person, circumstances, including self-identification, show the person answering to be the one called; or

   (B) In the case of a business, the call was made to a place of business and the conversation related to business reasonably transacted over the telephone;

(7) Evidence that a document authorized by law to be recorded or filed and in fact recorded or filed in a public office or a purported public record, report, statement, or data compilation, in any form, is from the public office where items of this nature are kept;

(8) Evidence that a document or data compilation, in any form:

   (A) Is in such condition as to create no suspicion concerning its authenticity;

   (B) Was in a place where it, if authentic, would likely be; and

   (C) Has been in existence 20 years or more at the time it is offered;

(9) Evidence describing a process or system used to produce a result and showing that the process or system produces an accurate result; or

(10) Any method of authentication or identification provided by law.

§ 24-9-902. Self-authentication

Extrinsic evidence of authenticity as a condition precedent to admissibility shall not be required with respect to the following:

(1) A document bearing a seal purporting to be that of the United States or of any state, district, commonwealth, territory, or insular possession thereof or the Panama Canal Zone or the Trust Territory of the Pacific Islands or of a political subdivision, department, officer, or agency thereof or of a municipal corporation of this state and bearing a signature purporting to be an attestation or execution;

(2) A document purporting to bear the signature in the official capacity of an officer or employee of any entity included in paragraph (1) of this Code section having no seal, if a public officer having a seal and having official duties in the district or political subdivision of the officer or employee certifies under seal that the signer has the official capacity and that the signature is genuine;

(3) A document purporting to be executed or attested in an official capacity by a person authorized by the laws of a foreign country to make such execution or attestation and accompanied by a final certification as to the genuineness of the signature, official position of the executing or attesting person, or of any foreign official whose certificate of genuineness of signature and official position relates to such execution or attestation or is in a chain of certificates of genuineness of signature and official position relating to such execution or attestation. A final certification may be made by a secretary of embassy or legation, consul general, consul, vice consul, or consular agent of the United States or a diplomatic or consular official of the foreign country assigned or accredited to the United States. If reasonable opportunity has been given to all parties to investigate the authenticity and accuracy of official documents, the court may, for good cause shown, order that such documents be treated as presumptively authentic without final certification or permit such documents to be evidenced by an attested summary with or without final certification;

(4) A duplicate of an official record or report or entry therein or of a document authorized by law to be recorded or filed and actually recorded or filed in a public office, including data compilations in any form, certified as correct by the custodian or other person authorized to make the certification by certificate complying with paragraph (1), (2), or (3) of this Code section or complying with any law of the United States or of this state, including Code Section 24-9-920;

(5) Books, pamphlets, or other publications purporting to be issued by a public office;

(6) Printed materials purporting to be newspapers or periodicals;

(7) Inscriptions, signs, tags, or labels purporting to have been affixed in the course of business and indicating ownership, control, or origin;

(8) Documents accompanied by a certificate of acknowledgment executed in the manner provided by law by a notary public or other officer authorized by law to take acknowledgments;

(9) Commercial paper, signatures thereon, and documents relating thereto to the extent provided by general commercial law;

§ 24-9-902(10). Self-authentication

(10) Any signature, document, or other matter declared by any law of the United States or of this state to be presumptively or prima facie genuine or authentic;

(11) The original or a duplicate of a domestic record of regularly conducted activity that would be admissible under paragraph (6) of Code Section 24-8-803 if accompanied by a written declaration of its custodian or other qualified person certifying that the record:

    (A) Was made at or near the time of the occurrence of the matters set forth by, or from information transmitted by, a person with knowledge of such matters;

    (B) Was kept in the course of the regularly conducted activity; and

    (C) Was made by the regularly conducted activity as a regular practice.

A party intending to offer a record into evidence under this paragraph shall provide written notice of such intention to all adverse parties and shall make the record and declaration available for inspection sufficiently in advance of their offer into evidence to provide an adverse party with a fair opportunity to challenge such record and declaration; or

(12) In a civil proceeding, the original or a duplicate of a foreign record of regularly conducted activity that would be admissible under paragraph (6) of Code Section 24-8-803 if accompanied by a written declaration by its custodian or other qualified person certifying that the record:

    (A) Was made at or near the time of the occurrence of the matters set forth by, or from information transmitted by, a person with knowledge of those matters;

    (B) Was kept in the course of the regularly conducted activity; and

    (C) Was made by the regularly conducted activity as a regular practice.

The declaration shall be signed in a manner that, if falsely made, would subject the maker to criminal penalty under the laws of the country where the declaration is signed. A party intending to offer a record into evidence under this paragraph shall provide written notice of such intention to all adverse parties and shall make the record and declaration available for inspection sufficiently in advance of their offer into evidence to provide an adverse party with a fair opportunity to challenge such record and declaration.

§ 24-9-903. Subscribing witness's testimony

The testimony of a subscribing witness shall not be necessary to authenticate a writing unless required by the laws of the jurisdiction whose laws govern the validity of the writing.

§ 24-9-904. Definitions

As used in this article, the term:

    (1) "Public office" shall have the same meaning as set forth in Code Section 24-8-801.

    (2) "Public officer" means any person appointed or elected to be the head of any entity included in paragraph (1) of Code Section 24-9-902.

    (3) "Telephone service provider" shall have the same meaning as "voice service provider" as set forth in Code Section 46-5-231.

Article 2. Specific Types of Records and Evidence

§ 24-9-920. Authentication of Georgia state and county records

The certificate or attestation of any public officer either of this state or any county thereof or any clerk or keeper of county, consolidated government, or municipal records in this state shall give sufficient validity or authenticity to any copy or transcript of any record, document, paper or file, or other matter or thing in such public officer's respective office, or pertaining thereto, to admit the same in evidence.

§ 24-9-921. Identification of medical bills; expert witness unnecessary

(a) Upon the trial of any civil proceeding involving injury or disease, the patient or the member of his or her family or other person responsible for the care of the patient shall be a competent witness to identify bills for expenses incurred in the treatment of the patient upon a showing by such a witness that the expenses were incurred in connection with the treatment of the injury, disease, or disability involved in the subject of litigation at trial and that the bills were received from:

  (1) A hospital;
  (2) An ambulance service;
  (3) A pharmacy, drugstore, or supplier of therapeutic or orthopedic devices; or
  (4) A licensed practicing physician, dentist, orthodontist, podiatrist, physical or occupational therapist, doctor of chiropractic, psychologist, advanced practice registered nurse, social worker, professional counselor, or marriage and family therapist.

(b) Such items of evidence need not be identified by the one who submits the bill, and it shall not be necessary for an expert witness to testify that the charges were reasonable and necessary. However, nothing in this Code section shall be construed to limit the right of a thorough and sifting cross-examination as to such items of evidence.

§ 24-9-922. Proof of laws, records, nonjudicial records, or books of other states, territories, or possessions; full faith and credit

The acts of the legislature of any other state, territory, or possession of the United States, the records and judicial proceedings of any court of any such state, territory, or possession, and the nonjudicial records or books kept in the public offices in any such state, territory, or possession, if properly authenticated, shall have the same full faith and credit in every court within this state as they have by law or usage in the courts of such state, territory, or possession from which they are taken.

§ 24-9-923. Authentication of photographs, motion pictures, video recordings, and audio recordings when witness unavailable

(a) As used in this Code section, the term "unavailability of a witness" includes situations in which the authenticating witness:
(1) Is exempted by ruling of the court on the ground of privilege from testifying concerning the subject matter of the authentication;
(2) Persists in refusing to testify concerning the subject matter of the authentication despite an order of the court to do so;
(3) Testifies to a lack of memory of the subject matter of the authentication;
(4) Is unable to be present or to testify at the hearing because of death or then existing physical or mental illness or infirmity; or
(5) Is absent from the hearing and the proponent of the authentication has been unable to procure the attendance of the authenticating witness by process or other reasonable means.

An authenticating witness shall not be deemed unavailable as a witness if his or her exemption, refusal, claim of lack of memory, inability, or absence is due to the procurement or wrongdoing of the proponent of an authentication for the purpose of preventing the witness from attending or testifying.
(b) Subject to any other valid objection, photographs, motion pictures, video recordings, and audio recordings shall be admissible in evidence when necessitated by the unavailability of a witness who can provide personal authentication and when the court determines, based on competent evidence presented to the court, that such items tend to show reliably the fact or facts for which the items are offered.
(c) Subject to any other valid objection, photographs, motion pictures, video recordings, and audio recordings produced at a time when the device producing the items was not being operated by an individual person or was not under the personal control or in the presence of an individual operator shall be admissible in evidence when the court determines, based on competent evidence presented to the court, that such items tend to show reliably the fact or facts for which the items are offered, provided that, prior to the admission of such evidence, the date and time of such photograph, motion picture, or video recording shall be contained on such evidence, and such date and time shall be shown to have been made contemporaneously with the events depicted in such photograph, motion picture, or video recording.
(d) This Code section shall not be the exclusive method of introduction into evidence of photographs, motion pictures, video recordings, and audio recordings but shall be supplementary to any other law and lawful methods existing in this state.

§ 24-9-924. Admissibility of records of Department of Driver Services; admissibility of computer transmitted records

(a) Any court may receive and use as evidence in any proceeding information otherwise admissible from the records of the Department of Public Safety or the Department of Driver Services obtained from any terminal lawfully connected to the Georgia Crime Information Center without the need for additional certification of such records.
(b) Any court may receive and use as evidence for the purpose of imposing a sentence in any criminal proceeding information otherwise admissible from the records of the Department of Driver Services obtained from a request made in accordance with a contract with the Georgia Technology Authority for immediate on-line electronic furnishing of information.

§ 24-10-1001. [Best Evidence] Definitions

Chapter 10. Best Evidence Rule

§ 24-10-1001. Definitions
As used in this chapter, the term:

(1) "Writing" or "recording" means letters, words, or numbers, or their equivalent, set down by handwriting, typewriting, printing, photostating, magnetic impulse, or mechanical or electronic recording or other form of data compilation.

(2) "Photograph" includes still photographs, X-ray films, video recordings, and motion pictures.

(3) "Original" means the writing or recording itself or any counterpart intended to have the same effect by a person executing or issuing it. An original of a photograph includes the negative or any print therefrom. If data are stored in a computer or similar device, any printout or other output readable by sight, shown to reflect the data accurately, is an original.

(4) "Duplicate" means a counterpart produced by the same impression as the original or from the same matrix or by means of photography, including enlargements and miniatures, or by mechanical or electronic rerecording, chemical reproduction, or other equivalent techniques which accurately reproduce the original.

(5) "Public record" shall have the same meaning as set forth in Code Section 24-8-801.

§ 24-10-1002. Requirement of original
To prove the contents of a writing, recording, or photograph, the original writing, recording, or photograph shall be required.

§ 24-10-1003. Admissibility of duplicates
A duplicate shall be admissible to the same extent as an original unless:

(1) A genuine question is raised as to the authenticity of the original; or

(2) A circumstance exists where it would be unfair to admit the duplicate in lieu of the original.

§ 24-10-1004. Admissibility of other evidence of contents of a writing, recording, or photograph
The original shall not be required and other evidence of the contents of a writing, recording, or photograph shall be admissible if:

(1) All originals are lost or have been destroyed, unless the proponent lost or destroyed them in bad faith;

(2) No original can be obtained by any available judicial process or procedure;

(3) At a time when an original was under the control of the party against whom offered, that party was put on notice, by the pleadings or otherwise, that the contents would be a subject of proof at the hearing, and that party does not produce the original at the hearing; or

(4) The writing, recording, or photograph is not closely related to a controlling issue.

§ 24-10-1005. Public records

The contents of a public record, or of a document authorized to be recorded or filed and actually recorded or filed, including data compilations in any form, if otherwise admissible, may be proved by duplicate, certified as correct in accordance with Code Section 24-9-902 or Code Section 24-9-920 or testified to be correct by a witness who has compared it with the original. If a duplicate which complies with this Code section cannot be obtained by the exercise of reasonable diligence, then other evidence of the contents may be given.

§ 24-10-1006. Summaries

The contents of otherwise admissible voluminous writings, recordings, or photographs which cannot conveniently be examined in court may be presented in the form of a chart, summary, or calculation. The originals, or duplicates, shall be made available for examination or copying, or both, by other parties at a reasonable time and place. The court may order that the contents of such writings, recordings, or photographs be produced in court.

§ 24-10-1007. Testimony or written admission of party

The contents of writings, recordings, or photographs may be proved by the testimony or deposition of the party against whom offered or by that party's written admission, without accounting for the nonproduction of the original.

§ 24-10-1008. Functions of court and jury

When the admissibility of other evidence of the contents of writings, recordings, or photographs under the rules of evidence depends upon the fulfillment of a condition of fact, the question of whether the condition has been fulfilled is ordinarily for the court to determine in accordance with the provisions of Code Section 24-1-104; provided, however, that when an issue is raised as to:

(1) Whether the asserted writing, recording, or photograph ever existed;
(2) Whether another writing, recording, or photograph produced at the trial is the original; or
(3) Whether other evidence of the contents correctly reflects the contents,

the issue is for the trier of fact to determine as in the case of other issues of fact.

Chapter 11. Establishment Of Lost Records

Article 1. Public Records

§ 24-11-1. Definitions

As used in this chapter, the term:

(1) "Custodian" means the person charged with the duty of maintaining public records.
(2) "Duplicate" means a counterpart which accurately reproduces the original.
(3) "Public record" shall have the same meaning as set forth in Code Section 24-8-801.

§ 24-11-2. Establishment of lost records

(a) Where any original public records have been lost, mutilated, stolen, or destroyed, the custodian may establish duplicates in accordance with the provisions of this article. When such public records are established by duplicates, they shall have all of the effect in evidence as the original records would have had.

(b) The custodian of the lost, mutilated, stolen, or destroyed public records shall bring a petition to establish such records in the superior court of the county in which the public records were located.

(c) The petition shall set forth the fact that some portion of the public records has been lost, mutilated, stolen, or destroyed, specifying as nearly as may be possible the books or parts of the books in which those records existed, and shall pray for the establishment of such records.

§ 24-11-3. Appointment of auditor; hearing; establishment of duplicates

(a) The court shall either appoint an auditor for such petition in accordance with Chapter 7 of Title 9 or shall conduct a hearing on the petition. If an auditor is appointed, the provisions of Code Sections 9-7-1 through 9-7-16 and Code Section 9-7-21 shall apply to such proceedings. An auditor shall receive compensation for services rendered as may be allowed by the court, to be paid out of the funds of the office of the custodian whose records were lost, mutilated, stolen, or destroyed.

(b) If the court hears the petition, after receiving evidence, the court shall determine whether the purported duplicate is, in fact, the same as the original record which has been lost, mutilated, stolen, or destroyed, and it shall be discretionary with the court to order the whole or any part of such records established. The court shall give precedence to a petition filed pursuant to this article and hear the petition as speedily as possible.

(c) The duplicates which are established pursuant to this Code section, as nearly as may be possible, shall specify and conform to the original book and pages of the same on which they originally existed.

Article 2. Private Papers

§ 24-11-20. Establishment of lost office papers

(a) Upon the loss of any original pleading, declaration, bill of indictment, special presentment, accusation, or other office paper, a duplicate may be established instanter on motion.

(b) As used in this article, the term "office paper" means the instrument upon which a proceeding has been brought after the case has gone to trial.

§ 24-11-21. Summary establishment of lost or destroyed evidence of indebtedness in probate court -- Petition; service of notice; hearing and decision; recordation; appeal to superior court

§ 24-11-21. Summary establishment of lost or destroyed evidence of indebtedness in probate court -- Petition; service of notice; hearing and decision; recordation; appeal to superior court

(a) The owner, agent of the owner, or legal representative of the owner of any bond, bill, note, draft, check, or other evidence of indebtedness which has been lost or destroyed may establish a duplicate of the same in a summary manner by filing a petition with the judge of the probate court of the county of the residence of the alleged debtor or maker, if he or she is a resident of this state; and the judge of the probate court shall be deemed a judicial officer for the purpose of this Code section. The petition shall be sworn to by the party applying and shall contain as full and accurate a description as possible of the lost paper, of the loss and mode of loss, and of the inability to find the same and why, along with a prayer for the establishment of a duplicate setting forth the duplicate desired to be established.

(b) Upon the filing of a petition, the judge shall issue a citation or notice to the alleged debtor or maker requiring the debtor or maker to appear at a day not more than ten days distant and show cause, if he or she has any, why the duplicate should not be established in lieu of the lost original. The citation or notice shall be personally served in the manner provided in Code Section 9-11-4 at least five days before the time of the hearing.

(c) If no successful defense is made at the time and place appointed, the judge shall proceed to establish, by an order entered on the petition, the duplicate so prayed to be established, which shall have all the effect of the original. The petition, notice, and order shall be entered in a book of record specially prepared for this purpose.

(d) If the debtor or maker files a defense under oath to the effect that the original never existed as claimed, the judge shall decide the case, after giving the parties time for preparation and hearing, not to exceed 20 days. If the judge's decision is in favor of the applicant and no appeal is entered as provided in subsection (e) of this Code section, the decision shall be entered on the petition, and the duplicate so established shall have the same effect as an original. If the judge's decision is in favor of the alleged debtor or maker, the judge shall also enter his or her decision on the petition. In all cases, the proceedings shall be recorded as provided in subsection (c) of this Code section.

(e) Except as provided in Article 6 of Chapter 9 of Title 15, if either party to the proceedings provided for in this Code section is dissatisfied, such party may appeal upon giving the usual bond and security for costs, as in cases of appeal from the probate court to the superior court. The appeal shall be tried in the superior court from all the pleadings and proceedings as were before the judge of the probate court. In the superior court, the case shall be tried and determined as provided in Code Sections 24-11-23 through 24-11-26.

(f) This Code section shall not apply to evidences of indebtedness to which Title 11, the "Uniform Commercial Code," is applicable.

§ 24-11-22. Summary establishment of lost or destroyed evidence of indebtedness in probate court -- Service of nonresidents; effect

When the person alleged to be a debtor or maker of a lost or destroyed paper as set forth in Code Section 24-11-21 does not reside in this state, the alleged debtor or maker may be made a party to the proceedings by publication, in a newspaper to be designated by the judge of the probate court, twice a month for two months. When the person has been made a party, this article shall apply in his or her case.

§ 24-11-23. Establishment of lost or destroyed paper in superior court -- Petition and affidavit; issuance and service of rule nisi

(a) The owner of a lost or destroyed paper which is not an office paper, as defined in Code Section 24-11-20, who desires to establish such paper shall present to the clerk of the superior court of the county where the maker of the paper resides, if the maker is a resident of this state, a petition in writing, together with a duplicate, in substance, of the paper lost or destroyed, as nearly as he or she can recollect, which duplicate shall be sworn to by the petitioner, the petitioner's agent, or the petitioner's attorney.

(b) The clerk shall issue a rule nisi in the name of the judge of the superior court calling upon the opposite party to show cause, if he or she has any, why the duplicate sworn to should not be established in lieu of the lost or destroyed original. If the respondent is found in this state, the rule nisi shall be served personally upon the respondent in the manner provided by Code Section 9-11-4 at least 20 days before the sitting of the court to which the rule nisi is made returnable. If the respondent cannot be found in this state, the rule nisi shall be served upon the respondent by publication in the manner provided in Code Section 9-11-4 before the final hearing of the rule nisi.

§ 24-11-24. Establishment of lost or destroyed paper in superior court -- When continuance granted

In a proceeding to establish lost papers under Code Section 24-11-23, no continuance shall be granted unless it appears reasonable and just to the court; nor shall a continuance be allowed to the same party more than once, except for providential cause.

§ 24-11-25. Establishment of lost or destroyed paper

When a rule nisi has been served as provided in Code Section 24-11-23, the court shall grant a rule absolute establishing the duplicate of the lost or destroyed paper sworn to, unless good and sufficient cause is shown why the rule absolute should not be granted.

§ 24-11-26. Establishment of lost or destroyed paper -- Furnishing of certified endorsement of copy

When the duplicate of the lost or destroyed paper is established, the clerk of the court in which it is done shall furnish the duplicate to the party who had it established, with a certified endorsement thereon of the day and term of the court when the rule absolute was granted, provided all costs of the proceeding have been paid.

§ 24-11-27. Procedure as to action on lost or destroyed note, bill, bond, or other instrument

(a) If the paper which has been lost or destroyed is a note, bill, bond, or other instrument upon which a proceeding may be brought, the owner may institute a proceeding thereon as soon as the rule nisi has been issued as provided for in Code Section 24-11-23. The complaint shall set forth that the paper upon which the proceeding is based is lost or destroyed. In no case shall a judgment be entered in the proceeding until it is determined whether the application to establish the paper is granted or not. If the application is granted, then judgment shall be entered as in other proceedings.

(b) In a proceeding as provided for in subsection (a) of this Code section, production of the paper upon which the proceeding is based shall not be demanded until the time for rendition of judgment in the proceeding; at that time, if the plaintiff produces a duplicate of the paper with a certified endorsement thereon by the clerk of the court in which it was established, as provided in Code Section 24-11-26, it shall be taken and considered as the original.

(c) This Code section shall not apply to instruments to which Title 11, the "Uniform Commercial Code," is applicable.

§ 24-11-28. Joinder of additional party defendants in proceedings to establish lost or destroyed papers

In all proceedings for the purpose of establishing any lost or destroyed paper other than an office paper, as defined in Code Section 24-11-20, any person whose interest will be affected by the establishment of the lost paper shall, upon motion, by order of the court, be made a party respondent in the proceeding and shall be allowed all the rights of defense against the establishment of the paper as fully as if he or she was the maker of the lost paper.

§ 24-11-29. Applicability of article

Other than Code Section 24-11-20, this article shall not apply to lost or destroyed papers to which Title 11, the "Uniform Commercial Code," is applicable.

§ 24-12-1. When medical information may be released by physician, hospital, health care facility, or pharmacist; immunity from liability; waiver of privilege; psychiatrists and hospitals excepted

Chapter 12. Medical And Other Confidential Information

Article 1. Release Of Medical Information and Confidentiality of Raw Research Data

§ 24-12-1. When medical information may be released by physician, hospital, health care facility, or pharmacist; immunity from liability; waiver of privilege; psychiatrists and hospitals excepted

(a) No physician licensed under Chapter 34 of Title 43 and no hospital or health care facility, including those operated by an agency or bureau of this state or other governmental unit, shall be required to release any medical information concerning a patient except to the Department of Public Health, its divisions, agents, or successors when required in the administration of public health programs pursuant to Code Section 31-12-2 and where authorized or required by law, statute, or lawful regulation; or on written authorization or other waiver by the patient, or by his or her parents or duly appointed guardian ad litem in the case of a minor, or on appropriate court order or subpoena; provided, however, that any physician, hospital, or health care facility releasing information under written authorization or other waiver by the patient, or by his or her parents or guardian ad litem in the case of a minor, or pursuant to law, statute, or lawful regulation, or under court order or subpoena shall not be liable to the patient or any other person; provided, further, that the privilege shall be waived to the extent that the patient places his or her care and treatment or the nature and extent of his or her injuries at issue in any judicial proceeding. This Code section shall not apply to psychiatrists or to hospitals in which the patient is being or has been treated solely for mental illness.

(b) No pharmacist licensed under Chapter 4 of Title 26 shall be required to release any medical information concerning a patient except on written authorization or other waiver by the patient, or by his or her parents or duly appointed guardian ad litem in the case of a minor, or upon appropriate court order or subpoena; provided, however, that any pharmacist releasing information under written authorization or other waiver by the patient, or by his or her parents or duly appointed guardian ad litem in the case of a minor, or upon appropriate court order or subpoena shall not be liable to the patient or any other person; provided, further, that the privilege shall be waived to the extent that the patient places his or her care and treatment or the nature and extent of his or her injuries at issue in any judicial proceeding.

§ 24-12-2. Confidentiality of raw research data

(a) The General Assembly finds and declares that protecting the confidentiality of research data from disclosure in judicial and administrative proceedings is essential to safeguarding the integrity of research in this state, guaranteeing the privacy of individuals who participate in research projects, and ensuring the continuation of research in science, medicine, and other fields that benefits the citizens and institutions of Georgia and other states. The protection of such research data has more than local significance, is of equal importance to all citizens of this state, is of state-wide concern, and consequently is properly a matter for regulation under the police power of this state.

(b) As used in this Code section, the term "confidential raw research data" means medical information, interview responses, reports, statements, memoranda, or other data relating to the condition, treatment, or characteristics of any person which are gathered by or provided to a researcher:

    (1) In support of a research study approved by an appropriate research oversight committee of a hospital, health care facility, or educational institution; and

    (2) With the objective to develop, study, or report aggregate or anonymous information not intended to be used in any way in which the identity of an individual is material to the results.

    The term shall not include published compilations of the raw research data created by the researcher or the researcher's published summaries, findings, analyses, or conclusions related to the research study.

(c) Confidential raw research data in a researcher's possession shall not be subject to subpoena, otherwise discoverable, or deemed admissible as evidence in any judicial or administrative proceeding in any court except as otherwise provided in subsection (d) of this Code section.

§ 24-12-2. Confidentiality of raw research data

(d) Confidential raw research data may be released, disclosed, subject to subpoena, otherwise discoverable, or deemed admissible as evidence in a judicial or administrative proceeding as follows:

(1) Confidential raw research data related to a person may be disclosed to that person or to another person on such person's behalf where the authority is otherwise specifically provided by law;

(2) Confidential raw research data related to a person may be disclosed to any person or legal entity designated to receive that information when that designation is made in writing by the research participant or where a designation is made in writing by a person authorized by law to act for the participant;

(3) Confidential raw research data related to a person may be disclosed to any agency or department of the federal government, this state, or any political subdivision of this state if such data are required by law or regulation to be reported to such agency or department;

(4) Confidential raw research data may be disclosed in any proceeding in which a party was a participant, researcher, or sponsor in the underlying research study, including, but not limited to, any judicial or administrative proceeding in which a research participant places his or her care, treatment, injuries, insurance coverage, or benefit plan coverage at issue; provided, however, that the identity of any research participant other than the party to the judicial or administrative proceeding shall not be disclosed, unless the researcher or sponsor is a defendant in such proceeding;

(5) Confidential raw research data may be disclosed in any judicial or administrative proceeding in which the researcher has either volunteered to testify or has been hired to testify as an expert by one of the parties to such proceeding; and

(6) In a criminal proceeding, the court shall order the production of confidential raw research data if the data are relevant to any issue in the proceeding, impose appropriate safeguards against unauthorized disclosure of the data, and admit confidential raw research data into evidence if the data are material to the defense or prosecution.

(e) Nothing in this Code section shall be construed to permit, require, or prohibit the disclosure of confidential raw research data in any setting other than a judicial or administrative proceeding that is governed by the requirements of this title.

(f) Any disclosure of confidential raw research data authorized or required by this Code section or any other law shall in no way destroy the confidential nature of that data except for the purpose for which the authorized or required disclosure is made.

Article 2. Confidentiality Of Medical Information

§ 24-12-10. Definitions

As used in this article, the term:

(1) "Confidential or privileged" means the protection afforded by law from unauthorized disclosure, whether the protection is afforded by law as developed and applied by the courts, by statute or lawful regulations, or by the requirements of the Constitutions of the State of Georgia or the United States. The term "confidential or privileged" also includes protection afforded by law from compulsory process or testimony.

(2) "Disclosure" means the act of transmitting or communicating medical matter to a person who would not otherwise have access thereto.

(3) "Health care facility" means any institution or place in which health care is rendered to persons, which health care includes, but is not limited to, medical, psychiatric, acute, intermediate, rehabilitative, and long-term care.

(4) "Laws requiring disclosure" means laws and statutes of the State of Georgia and of the United States and lawful regulations issued by any department or agency of the State of Georgia or of the United States which require the review, analysis, or use of medical matter by persons not originally having authorized access thereto. The term "laws requiring disclosure" also includes any authorized practice of disclosure for purposes of evaluating claims for reimbursement for charges or expenses under any public or private reimbursement or insurance program.

(5) "Limited consent to disclosure" means proper authorization given by or on behalf of a person entitled to protection from disclosure of medical matter and given for a specific purpose related to such person's health or related to such person's application for insurance or like benefits.

(6) "Medical matter" means information respecting the medical or psychiatric condition, including without limitation the physical and the mental condition, of a natural person or persons, however recorded, obtained, or communicated.

(7) "Nurse" means a person authorized by license issued under Chapter 26 of Title 43 as a registered professional nurse or licensed practical nurse to practice nursing.

(8) "Physician" means any person lawfully licensed in this state to practice medicine and surgery pursuant to Chapter 34 of Title 43.

§ 24-12-11. Disclosure of medical records -- Effect on confidential or privileged character thereof

The disclosure of confidential or privileged medical matter constituting all or part of a record kept by a health care facility, a nurse, or a physician, pursuant to laws requiring disclosure or pursuant to limited consent to disclosure, shall not serve to destroy or in any way abridge the confidential or privileged character thereof, except for the purpose for which such disclosure is made.

§ 24-12-12. Disclosure of medical records -- Use of medical matter disclosed
Persons to whom confidential or privileged medical matter is disclosed in the circumstances described in Code Section 24-12-11 shall utilize such matter only in connection with the purpose or purposes of such disclosure and thereafter shall keep such matter in confidence. However, nothing in this article shall prohibit the use of such matter where otherwise authorized by law.

§ 24-12-13. Disclosure of medical records -- Immunity from liability
Any person, corporation, authority, or other legal entity acting in good faith shall be immune from liability for the transmission, receipt, or use of medical matter disclosed pursuant to laws requiring disclosure or pursuant to limited consent to disclosure.

§ 24-12-14. Disclosure of medical records -- Use for educational purposes not precluded
Nothing in this article shall be construed to prevent the customary and usual audit, discussion, and presentation of cases in connection with medical and public education.

Article 3. Aids Information

§ 24-12-20. Confidential nature of AIDS information
AIDS confidential information as defined in Code Section 31-22-9.1 and disclosed or discovered within the patient-physician relationship shall be confidential and shall not be disclosed except as otherwise provided in Code Section 24-12-21.

§ 24-12-21. Disclosure of AIDS confidential information
(a) Any term used in this Code section and defined in Code Section 31-22-9.1 shall have the meaning provided for such term in Code Section 31-22-9.1.
(b) Except as otherwise provided in this Code section:
    (1) No person or legal entity which receives AIDS confidential information pursuant to this Code section or which is responsible for recording, reporting, or maintaining AIDS confidential information shall:
        (A) Intentionally or knowingly disclose that information to another person or legal entity; or
        (B) Be compelled by subpoena, court order, or other judicial process to disclose that information to another person or legal entity; and
    (2) No person or legal entity which receives AIDS confidential information which that person or legal entity knows was disclosed in violation of paragraph (1) of this subsection shall:
        (A) Intentionally or knowingly disclose that information to another person or legal entity; or
        (B) Be compelled by subpoena, court order, or other judicial process to disclose that information to another person or legal entity.

§ 24-12-21. Disclosure of AIDS confidential information

(c) AIDS confidential information shall be disclosed to the person identified by that information or, if that person is an incompetent person, to that person's legal guardian. AIDS confidential information may be disclosed to such person's parent or legal guardian if that person is a minor.

(d) AIDS confidential information shall be disclosed to any person or legal entity designated to receive that information when that designation is made in writing by the person identified by that information or, if that person is a minor or incompetent person, by that person's parent or legal guardian.

(e) AIDS confidential information shall be disclosed to any agency or department of the federal government, this state, or any political subdivision of this state if that information is authorized or required by law to be reported to that agency or department.

(f) The results of an HIV test shall be disclosed to the person, or that person's designated representative, who ordered such tests of the body fluids or tissue of another person.

(g) When the patient of a physician has been determined to be infected with HIV and that patient's physician reasonably believes that the spouse or sexual partner or any child of the patient, spouse, or sexual partner is a person at risk of being infected with HIV by that patient, the physician may disclose to that spouse, sexual partner, or child that the patient has been determined to be infected with HIV, after first attempting to notify the patient that such disclosure is going to be made.

(h)

(1) An administrator of an institution licensed as a hospital by the Department of Community Health or a physician having a patient who has been determined to be infected with HIV may disclose to the Department of Public Health:

(A) The name and address of that patient;

(B) That such patient has been determined to be infected with HIV; and

(C) The name and address of any other person whom the disclosing physician or administrator reasonably believes to be a person at risk of being infected with HIV by that patient.

(2) When mandatory and nonanonymous reporting of confirmed positive HIV tests to the Department of Public Health is determined by that department to be reasonably necessary, that department shall establish by regulation a date on and after which such reporting shall be required. On and after the date so established, each health care provider, health care facility, or any other person or legal entity which orders an HIV test for another person shall report to the Department of Public Health the name and address of any person thereby determined to be infected with HIV. No such report shall be made regarding any confirmed positive HIV test provided at any anonymous HIV test site operated by or on behalf of the Department of Public Health.

(3) The Department of Public Health may disclose that a person has been reported, under paragraph (1) or (2) of this subsection, to have been determined to be infected with HIV to the board of health of the county in which that person resides or is located if reasonably necessary to protect the health and safety of that person or other persons who may have come in contact with the body fluids of the HIV infected person. The Department of

§ 24-12-21. Disclosure of AIDS confidential information

Public Health or county board of health to which information is disclosed pursuant to this paragraph or paragraph (1) or (2) of this subsection:

(A) May contact any person named in such disclosure as having been determined to be an HIV infected person for the purpose of counseling that person and requesting therefrom the name of any other person who may be a person at risk of being infected with HIV by that HIV infected person;

(B) May contact any other person reasonably believed to be a person at risk of being infected with HIV by that HIV infected person for the purposes of disclosing that such infected person has been determined to be infected with HIV and counseling such person to submit to an HIV test; and

(C) Shall contact and provide counseling to the spouse of any HIV infected person whose name is thus disclosed if both persons are reasonably likely to have engaged in sexual intercourse or any other act determined by the Department of Public Health likely to have resulted in the transmission of HIV between such persons within the preceding seven years and if that spouse may be located and contacted without undue difficulty.

(h.1) The Department of Public Health may disclose AIDS confidential information regarding a person who has been reported, under paragraph (1) or (2) of subsection (h), to be infected with HIV to a health care provider licensed pursuant to Chapter 11, 26, or 34 of Title 43 whom that person has consulted for medical treatment or advice.

(i) Any health care provider authorized to order an HIV test may disclose AIDS confidential information regarding a patient thereof if that disclosure is made to a health care provider or health care facility which has provided, is providing, or will provide any health care service to that patient and as a result of such provision of service that health care provider or facility:

(1) Has personnel or patients who may be persons at risk of being infected with HIV by that patient, if that patient is an HIV infected person and such disclosure is reasonably necessary to protect any such personnel or patients from that risk; or

(2) Has a legitimate need for that information in order to provide that health care service to that patient.

(j) A health care provider or any other person or legal entity authorized but not required to disclose AIDS confidential information pursuant to this Code section shall have no duty to make such disclosure and shall not be liable to the patient or any other person or legal entity for failing to make such disclosure. A health care provider or any other person or legal entity which discloses information as authorized or required by this Code section or as authorized or required by law or rules or regulations made pursuant thereto shall have no civil or criminal liability therefor.

(k) When any person or legal entity is authorized or required by this Code section or any other law to disclose AIDS confidential information to a person at risk of being infected with HIV and that person at risk is a minor or incompetent person, such disclosure may be made to any parent or legal guardian of the minor or incompetent person, to the minor or incompetent person, or to both the minor or incompetent person and any parent or legal guardian thereof.

§ 24-12-21. Disclosure of AIDS confidential information

(l) When an institutional care facility is the site at which a person is at risk of being infected with HIV and as a result of that risk a disclosure of AIDS confidential information to any person at risk at that site is authorized or required under this Code section or any other law, such disclosure may be made to the person at risk or to that institutional care facility's chief administrative or executive officer, or such officer's designee, in which case that officer or designee shall be authorized to make such disclosure to the person at risk.

(m) When a disclosure of AIDS confidential information is authorized or required by this Code section to be made to a physician, health care provider, or legal entity, that disclosure may be made to employees of that physician, health care provider, or legal entity who have been designated thereby to receive such information on behalf thereof. Those designated employees may thereafter disclose to and provide for the disclosure of that information among such other employees of that physician, health care provider, or legal entity, but such disclosures among those employees shall only be authorized when reasonably necessary in the ordinary course of business to carry out the purposes for which that disclosure is authorized or required to be made to that physician, health care provider, or legal entity.

(n) Any disclosure of AIDS confidential information authorized or required by this Code section or any other law and any unauthorized disclosure of such information shall in no way destroy the confidential nature of that information except for the purpose for which the authorized or required disclosure is made.

(o) Any person or legal entity which violates subsection (b) of this Code section shall be guilty of a misdemeanor.

(p) Nothing in this Code section or any other law shall be construed to authorize the disclosure of AIDS confidential information if that disclosure is prohibited by federal law, or regulations promulgated thereunder, nor shall anything in this Code section or any other law be construed to prohibit the disclosure of information which would be AIDS confidential information except that such information does not permit the identification of any person.

(q) A public safety agency or prosecuting attorney may obtain the results from an HIV test to which the person named in the request has submitted under Code Section 15-11-603, 17-10-15, 42-5-52.1, or 42-9-42.1, notwithstanding that the results may be contained in a sealed record.

(r) Any person or legal entity required by an order of a court to disclose AIDS confidential information in the custody or control of such person or legal entity shall disclose that information as required by that order.

(s) AIDS confidential information shall be disclosed as medical information pursuant to Code Section 24-12-1 or pursuant to any other law which authorizes or requires the disclosure of medical information if:

    (1) The person identified by that information:

        (A) Has consented in writing to that disclosure;

        (B) Has been notified of the request for disclosure of that information at least ten days prior to the time the disclosure is to be made and does not object to such disclosure prior to the time specified for that disclosure in that notice; or

        (C) Is suspected of being mentally ill and is the subject of an order issued pursuant to Code Section 37-3-41 when the court issuing such

§ 24-12-21. Disclosure of AIDS confidential information

order finds in an in camera hearing by clear and convincing evidence a compelling need for the information which cannot be accommodated by other means. In assessing compelling need, the court shall weigh the public health, safety, or welfare needs or any other public or private need for the disclosure against the privacy interest of the person identified by the information and the public interest which may be disserved by disclosures which may deter voluntary HIV tests. If the court determines that disclosure of that information is authorized under this subparagraph, the court shall order that disclosure and impose appropriate safeguards against any unauthorized disclosure. The records of that hearing otherwise shall be under seal; or

(2) A superior court in an in camera hearing finds by clear and convincing evidence a compelling need for the information which cannot be accommodated by other means. In assessing compelling need, the court shall weigh the public health, safety, or welfare needs or any other public or private need for the disclosure against the privacy interest of the person identified by the information and the public interest which may be disserved by disclosures which may deter voluntary HIV tests. If the court determines that disclosure of that information is authorized under this paragraph, the court shall order that disclosure and impose appropriate safeguards against any unauthorized disclosure. The records of that hearing otherwise shall be under seal.

(t)

(1) A superior court of this state may order a person or legal entity to disclose AIDS confidential information in its custody or control to:

(A) A prosecutor in connection with a prosecution for the alleged commission of reckless conduct under subsection (c) of Code Section 16-5-60;

(B) Any party in a civil proceeding; or

(C) A public safety agency or the Department of Public Health if that agency or department has an employee thereof who has, in the course of that employment, come in contact with the body fluids of the person identified by the AIDS confidential information sought in such a manner reasonably likely to cause that employee to become an HIV infected person and provided the disclosure is necessary for the health and safety of that employee,

and, for purposes of this subsection, the term "petitioner for disclosure" means any person or legal entity specified in subparagraph (A), (B), or (C) of this paragraph.

(2) An order may be issued against a person or legal entity responsible for recording, reporting, or maintaining AIDS confidential information to compel the disclosure of that information if the petitioner for disclosure demonstrates by clear and convincing evidence a compelling need for the information which cannot be accommodated by other means. In assessing compelling need, the court shall weigh the public health, safety, or welfare needs or any other public or private need for the disclosure against the privacy interest of the person identified by the information and the public interest which may be disserved by disclosures which may deter voluntary HIV tests.

§ 24-12-21. Disclosure of AIDS confidential information

(3) A petition seeking disclosure of AIDS confidential information under this subsection shall substitute a pseudonym for the true name of the person concerning whom the information is sought. The disclosure to the parties of that person's true name shall be communicated confidentially, in documents not filed with the court.

(4) Before granting any order under this subsection, the court shall provide the person concerning whom the information is sought with notice and a reasonable opportunity to participate in the proceedings if that person is not already a party.

(5) Court proceedings as to disclosure of AIDS confidential information under this subsection shall be conducted in camera unless the person concerning whom the information is sought agrees to a hearing in open court.

(6) Upon the issuance of an order that a person or legal entity be required to disclose AIDS confidential information regarding a person named in that order, that person or entity so ordered shall disclose to the ordering court any such information which is in the control or custody of that person or entity and which relates to the person named in the order for the court to make an in camera inspection thereof. If the court determines from that inspection that the person named in the order is an HIV infected person, the court shall disclose to the petitioner for disclosure that determination and shall impose appropriate safeguards against unauthorized disclosure which shall specify the persons who may have access to the information, the purposes for which the information shall be used, and appropriate prohibitions on future disclosure.

(7) The record of the proceedings under this subsection shall be sealed by the court.

(8) An order may not be issued under this subsection against the Department of Public Health, any county board of health, or any anonymous HIV test site operated by or on behalf of that department.

(u) A health care provider, health care facility, or other person or legal entity who, in violation of this Code section, unintentionally discloses AIDS confidential information, notwithstanding the maintenance of procedures thereby which are reasonably adopted to avoid risk of such disclosure, shall not be civilly or criminally liable, unless such disclosure was due to gross negligence or wanton and willful misconduct.

(v) AIDS confidential information may be disclosed when that disclosure is otherwise authorized or required by Code Section 42-1-6, if AIDS or HIV infection is the communicable disease at issue, or when that disclosure is otherwise authorized or required by any law which specifically refers to "AIDS confidential information," "HIV test results," or any similar language indicating a legislative intent to disclose information specifically relating to AIDS or HIV.

(w) A health care provider who has received AIDS confidential information regarding a patient from the patient's health care provider directly or indirectly under the provisions of subsection (i) of this Code section may disclose that information to a health care provider which has provided, is providing, or will provide any health care service to that patient and as a result of that provision of service that health care provider:

§ 24-12-21. Disclosure of AIDS confidential information

(1) Has personnel or patients who may be persons at risk of being infected with HIV by that patient, if that patient is an HIV infected person and such disclosure is reasonably necessary to protect any such personnel or patients from that risk; or

(2) Has a legitimate need for that information in order to provide that health care service to that patient.

(x) Neither the Department of Public Health nor any county board of health shall disclose AIDS confidential information contained in its records unless such disclosure is authorized or required by this Code section or any other law, except that such information in those records shall not be a public record and shall not be subject to disclosure through subpoena, court order, or other judicial process.

(y) The protection against disclosure provided by Code Section 24-12-20 shall be waived and AIDS confidential information may be disclosed to the extent that the person identified by such information, his or her heirs, successors, assigns, or a beneficiary of such person, including, but not limited to, an executor, administrator, or personal representative of such person's estate:

(1) Files a claim or claims other entitlements under any insurance policy or benefit plan or is involved in any civil proceeding regarding such claim;

(2) Places such person's care and treatment, the nature and extent of his or her injuries, the extent of his or her damages, his or her medical condition, or the reasons for his or her death at issue in any judicial proceeding; or

(3) Is involved in a dispute regarding coverage under any insurance policy or benefit plan.

(z) AIDS confidential information may be collected, used, and disclosed by an insurer in accordance with the provisions of Chapter 39 of Title 33.

(aa) In connection with any judicial proceeding in which AIDS confidential information is disclosed as authorized or required by this Code section, the party to whom that information is thereby disclosed may subpoena any person to authenticate such AIDS confidential information, establish a chain of custody relating thereto, or otherwise testify regarding that information, including, but not limited to, testifying regarding any notifications to the patient regarding results of an HIV test. The provisions of this subsection shall apply to records, personnel, or both of the Department of Public Health or a county board of health notwithstanding Code Section 50-18-72, but only as to test results obtained by a prosecutor under subsection (q) of this Code section and to be used thereby in a prosecution for reckless conduct under subsection (c) of Code Section 16-5-60.

(bb) AIDS confidential information may be disclosed as a part of any proceeding or procedure authorized or required pursuant to Chapter 3, 4, or 7 of Title 37, regarding a person who is alleged to be or who is mentally ill, developmentally disabled, or alcoholic or drug dependent, or as a part of any proceeding or procedure authorized or required pursuant to Title 29, regarding the guardianship of a person or that person's estate, as follows:

§ 24-12-21. Disclosure of AIDS confidential information

(1) Any person who files or transmits a petition or other document which discloses AIDS confidential information in connection with any such proceeding or procedure shall provide a cover page which contains only the type of proceeding or procedure, the court in which the proceeding or procedure is or will be pending, and the words "CONFIDENTIAL INFORMATION" without in any way otherwise disclosing thereon the name of any individual or that such petition or other document specifically contains AIDS confidential information;

(2) AIDS confidential information shall only be disclosed pursuant to this subsection after disclosure to and with the written consent of the person identified by that information, or that person's parent or guardian if that person is a minor or has previously been adjudicated as being incompetent, or by order of court obtained in accordance with subparagraph (C) of paragraph (3) of this subsection;

(3) If any person files or transmits a petition or other document in connection with any such proceeding or procedure which discloses AIDS confidential information without obtaining consent as provided in paragraph (2) of this subsection, the court receiving such information shall either obtain written consent as set forth in that paragraph (2) for any further use or disclosure of such information or:

(A) Return such petition or other document to the person who filed or transmitted same, with directions against further filing or transmittal of such information in connection with such proceeding or procedure except in compliance with this subsection;

(B) Delete or expunge all references to such AIDS confidential information from the particular petition or other document; or

(C)

(i) If the court determines there is a compelling need for such information in connection with the particular proceeding or procedure, petition a superior court of competent jurisdiction for permission to obtain or disclose that information. If the person identified by the information is not yet represented by an attorney in the proceeding or procedure in connection with which the information is sought, the petitioning court shall appoint an attorney for such person. The petitioning court shall have both that person and that person's attorney personally served with notice of the petition and time and place of the superior court hearing thereon. Such hearing shall not be held sooner than 72 hours after service, unless the information is to be used in connection with an emergency guardianship proceeding under Code Section 29-4-14, in which event the hearing shall not be held sooner than 48 hours after service.

(ii) The superior court in which a petition is filed pursuant to division (i) of this subparagraph shall hold an in camera hearing on such petition. The purpose of the hearing shall be to determine whether there is clear and convincing evidence of a compelling need for the AIDS confidential information sought in connection with the particular proceeding or procedure which cannot be accommodated by other means. In assessing compelling need, the superior court shall weigh the public health, safety, or welfare needs or any other public or private need for the disclosure against the privacy interest of the person identified by the information and the public interest which may be disserved by disclosures which may deter voluntary HIV tests. If the court determines that disclosure of that information is authorized under this subparagraph, the court shall order that disclosure and impose appropriate safeguards against any unauthorized disclosure. The records of that hearing otherwise shall be under seal; and

(4) The court having jurisdiction over such proceeding or procedure, when it becomes apparent that AIDS confidential information will likely be or has been disclosed in connection with such proceeding or procedure, shall take such measures as the court determines appropriate to preserve the confidentiality of the disclosed information to the maximum extent possible. Such measures shall include, without being limited to, closing the proceeding or procedure to the public and sealing all or any part of the records of the proceeding or procedure containing AIDS confidential information. The records of any appeals taken from any such proceeding or procedure shall also be sealed. Furthermore, the court may consult with and obtain the advice of medical experts or other counsel or advisers as to the relevance and materiality of such information in such proceedings or procedures, provided that the identity of the person identified by such information is not thereby revealed.

Article 4. Other Confidential Information

§ 24-12-30. Confidential nature of certain library records

(a) Circulation and similar records of a library which identify the user of library materials shall not be public records but shall be confidential and shall not be disclosed except:

(1) To members of the library staff in the ordinary course of business;

(2) Upon written consent of the user of the library materials or the user's parents or guardian if the user is a minor or ward; or

(3) Upon appropriate court order or subpoena.

(b) Any disclosure authorized by subsection (a) of this Code section or any unauthorized disclosure of materials made confidential by subsection (a) of this Code section shall not in any way destroy the confidential nature of that material, except for the purpose for which an authorized disclosure is made. A person disclosing material as authorized by subsection (a) of this Code section shall not be liable therefor.

§ 24-12-31. Confidential nature of veterinarian records; disclosure of rabies vaccination record

(a) No veterinarian licensed under Chapter 50 of Title 43 shall be required to disclose any information concerning the veterinarian's care of an animal except on written authorization or other waiver by the veterinarian's client or on appropriate court order or subpoena. Any veterinarian releasing information under written authorization or other waiver by the client or under court order or subpoena shall not be liable to the client or any other person. The confidentiality provided by this Code section shall be waived to the extent that the veterinarian's client places the veterinarian's care and treatment of the animal or the nature and extent of injuries to the animal at issue in any judicial proceeding. As used in this Code section, the term "client" means the owner of the animal or, if the owner of the animal is unknown, the person who presents the animal to the veterinarian for care and treatment.

(b) Notwithstanding the provisions of subsection (a) of this Code section, a veterinarian shall disclose the rabies vaccination history of any animal within such veterinarian's care within 24 hours of receipt of a written request by the physician of any person bitten by such animal.

Chapter 13. Securing Attendance of Witnesses and Production and Preservation of Evidence

§ 24-13-1. Freedom of witnesses from arrest

A witness shall not be arrested on any civil process while attending any court to which he or she is subpoenaed or otherwise required to attend as a witness or while going to or returning from such court. An officer who holds such witness imprisoned after seeing his or her subpoena or being satisfied of the fact that such person was a witness shall be liable for false imprisonment.

§ 24-13-2. Procedure for claiming witness fees

A witness in making a claim or proof of a claim for witness fees for attendance shall indicate the date on which he or she attended and, in the event of a continuance, shall not claim or receive witness fees for any day after the date to which the docket shows the proceeding was continued nor for any day before the continuance was granted on which he or she did not attend.

§ 24-13-3. Witness fee exceptions

(a) A witness shall not receive any witness fees for attendance on a subpoena if such witness is absent from the proceeding, or if the proceeding is continued at any time due to his or her absence, where such absence did not arise from providential cause.

(b) No witness shall receive witness fees from both parties in the same proceeding; the fees of a witness for both parties shall be apportioned equally between the parties unless the costs are all taxed against one party.

§ 24-13-4. Penalty for excessive witness fee claim

A witness who claims more than is due to such witness shall forfeit all witness fees and shall pay to the injured party, in addition thereto, four times the amount so unjustly claimed.

§ 24-13-5. Production of evidence when item not available; oath

When any person is served with a subpoena for the production of evidence or a notice to produce, seeking books in his or her possession to be used as testimony on the trial of any cause, if the person makes oath that he or she cannot produce the books required without suffering a material injury in his or her business and also makes or causes to be made out a full transcript from the books of all the accounts and dealings with the opposite party, has the transcript examined and sworn to by an impartial witness, and produces the same in court, the witness shall be deemed to have complied with the notice to produce or subpoena for the production of evidence.

§ 24-13-6. Procedure when adverse party dissatisfied with response pursuant to Code Section 24-13-5

When the transcript provided for in Code Section 24-13-5 is produced in court, if the adverse party is dissatisfied therewith and swears that he or she believes that the books contain entries material to the adverse party which do not appear in the transcript, the court shall grant him or her a commission directed to certain persons named by the parties and approved by the court. The commission shall cause the person with possession of the books to produce the books required with the person swearing that the books produced are all that he or she has or had that answer to the description in the subpoena or notice to produce. The commission shall examine the books and transmit to the court a full and fair statement of the accounts and entries between the parties under their hand. When received by the court, the statement of the commission shall be deemed a compliance with the notice to produce or subpoena for the production of evidence.

§ 24-13-7. Withdrawal of originals introduced in evidence; substitution of copies; discretion of court

Parties interested and participating in the trial of all cases tried in the courts are authorized and empowered, on the order of the court trying the case, to withdraw from the court and record of the case all original deeds, maps, blueprints, notes, papers, and documents belonging to the parties and which are introduced in evidence on the trial, on substituting therefor, when required by the court, duplicates thereof, verified as such by the parties or their agents, representatives, or attorneys. However, if any such deeds, maps, blueprints, notes, papers, or documents shall be attacked by any party to the case as forgeries, or as not being genuine originals, it shall be in the discretion of the court to require the original deeds, maps, blueprints, notes, papers, or documents so attacked to remain on file in the court as a part of the record in the case.

Article 2. Subpoenas And Notice to Produce

§ 24-13-20. Applicability
This article shall apply to all civil proceedings and, insofar as consistent with the Constitution, to all criminal proceedings.

§ 24-13-21. Subpoena for attendance of witnesses -- Form; issuance; subpoena in blank
(a) As used in this Code section, the term "subpoena" includes a witness subpoena and a subpoena for the production of evidence.
(b) A subpoena shall state the name of the court, the name of the clerk, and the title of the proceeding and shall command each person to whom it is directed to attend and give testimony or produce evidence at a time and place specified by the subpoena.
(c) The clerk of court shall make subpoenas in blank available on demand by electronic or other means to parties or their counsel or to the grand jury.
(d) An attorney who is counsel of record in a proceeding may issue and sign a subpoena obtained by electronic or other means from the clerk of court as an officer of a court for any deposition, hearing, or trial held in conjunction with such proceeding.
(e) A district attorney may issue, and upon the request of the grand jury shall issue, a subpoena in grand jury proceedings.
(f) A subpoena shall be completed prior to being served.
(g) Subpoenas are enforceable as provided in Code Section 24-13-26.
(h) If an individual misuses a subpoena, he or she shall be subject to punishment for contempt of court and shall be punished by a fine of not more than $300.00 or not more than 20 days' imprisonment, or both.

§ 24-13-22. Subpoena for attendance of witnesses -- Attendance at hearing or trial; where served
At the request of any party, subpoenas for attendance at a hearing or trial shall be issued under the authority of the clerk of the court in which the hearing or trial is held. A subpoena requiring the attendance of a witness at a hearing or trial may be served at any place within this state.

§ 24-13-23. Subpoena for production of documentary evidence; motion to quash or modify
(a) A subpoena may also command the person to whom it is directed to produce the evidence designated therein.
(b) The court, upon written motion made promptly and in any event at or before the time specified in the subpoena for compliance therewith, may:
(1) Quash or modify the subpoena if it is unreasonable and oppressive; or
(2) Condition denial of the motion upon the advancement by the person in whose behalf the subpoena is issued of the reasonable cost of producing the evidence.

§ 24-13-24. Service of subpoenas
A subpoena may be served by any sheriff, by his or her deputy, or by any other person not less than 18 years of age. Proof may be shown by return or certificate endorsed on a copy of the subpoena. Subpoenas may also be served by registered or certified mail or statutory overnight delivery, and the return receipt shall constitute prima-facie proof of service. Service upon a party may be made by serving his or her counsel of record.

§ 24-13-25. Fees and mileage; when tender required
Except as provided in Code Section 24-13-28, the witness fee shall be $25.00 per diem, and execution shall be issued by the clerk upon affidavit of the witness to enforce payment thereof. The payment of witness fees shall not be demanded as a condition precedent to attendance; but, when a witness resides outside the county where the testimony is to be given, service of the subpoena, to be valid, shall be accompanied by tender of the witness fee for one day's attendance plus mileage of 45 cent(s) per mile for traveling expenses for going from and returning to his or her place of residence by the nearest practical route. Tender of witness fees and mileage may be made by United States currency, postal money order, cashier's check, certified check, or the check of an attorney or law firm. When the subpoena is issued on behalf of this state, or an officer, agency, or political subdivision thereof, or an accused in a criminal proceeding, witness fees and mileage need not be tendered.

§ 24-13-26. Enforcement of subpoenas; continuance; secondary evidence of books, papers, or documents
(a) Subpoenas may be enforced by attachment for contempt and by a fine of not more than $300.00 or not more than 20 days' imprisonment, or both. In all proceedings under this Code section, the court shall consider whether under the circumstances of each proceeding the subpoena was served within a reasonable time, but in any event not less than 24 hours prior to the time that appearance thereunder was required.
(b) The court may also in appropriate proceedings grant continuance of the proceeding. Where subpoenas were issued in blank, no continuance shall be granted because of failure to respond thereto when the party obtaining such subpoenas fails to present to the clerk the name and address of the witness so subpoenaed at least six hours before appearance is required.
(c) When evidence is unsuccessfully sought, secondary evidence thereof shall be admissible.

§ 24-13-27. Notice to produce
Where a party desires to compel production of evidence in the possession, custody, or control of another party, in lieu of serving a subpoena under this article, the party desiring the production may serve a notice to produce upon counsel for the other party. Service may be perfected in accordance with Code Section 24-13-24, but no witness fees or mileage shall be allowed therefor. Such notices may be enforced in the manner prescribed by Code Section 24-13-26, and Code Section 24-13-23 shall also apply to such notices. The notice shall be in writing, signed by the party seeking production of the evidence, or the party's attorney, and shall be directed to the opposite party or his or her attorney.

§ 24-13-28. Witness fees for law enforcement officers

(a) As used in this Code section, the term:

(1) "Director" means the appropriate chief of police, sheriff, director of public safety of a college or university, local fire chief, director of the Georgia Bureau of Investigation, the commanding officer of the Georgia State Patrol, the commissioner of natural resources, the superintendent of a correctional institution, or the state fire marshal.

(2) "Law enforcement officer" means any member of a municipal or county police force, any deputy sheriff, any campus policeman as defined in Code Section 20-8-1, any member of a local fire department, any member of the Georgia State Patrol or Georgia Bureau of Investigation, any correctional officer, any person employed by the Department of Natural Resources as a law enforcement officer, or any arson investigator of the state fire marshal's office.

(3) "Regular duty hours" means the daily shift of duty to which a law enforcement officer is assigned and shall not include paid or unpaid vacation, paid or unpaid sick leave, paid or unpaid holiday leave, or any other paid or unpaid leave status established pursuant to the personnel regulations or scheduling practices of the employing agency.

(b) Any law enforcement officer who shall be required by subpoena to attend any superior court, other courts having jurisdiction to enforce the penal laws of this state, municipal court having jurisdiction to enforce the penal laws of this state as provided by Code Section 40-13-21, juvenile court, grand jury, hearing or inquest held or called by a coroner, or magistrate court involving any criminal matter, as a witness on behalf of the state during any hours except the regular duty hours to which the officer is assigned, shall be paid for such attendance at a fixed rate to be established by the governing authority, but not less than $25.00 per diem. The claim for the witness fees shall be endorsed on the subpoena showing the dates of attendance and stating that attendance was required during the hours other than the regular duty hours to which the claimant was assigned. The claimant shall verify this statement. The dates of attendance shall be certified by the judge or the prosecuting attorney of the court attended. The director or his or her designee shall certify that the claimant has not received any overtime pay for his or her attendance and that his or her attendance was required during hours other than regular duty hours. The amount due shall be paid by the governing body authorized to dispense public funds for the operation of the court. However, no such law enforcement officer shall claim or receive more than one witness fee per day for attendance in any court or before the grand jury regardless of the number of subpoenas which the law enforcement officer may have received requiring such officer to appear in such court or before the grand jury on any one day.

(c)
    (1) Except as provided in paragraph (2) of this subsection, any law enforcement officer who shall be required by subpoena to attend any court of this state with respect to any civil proceeding, as a witness concerning any matter relative to the law enforcement duties of such law enforcement officer during any hours except the regular duty hours to which the law enforcement officer is assigned, shall be paid for such attendance at a fixed rate to be established by the governing authority, but not less than $25.00 per diem. Any such law enforcement officer shall also be entitled to the mileage allowance provided in Code Section 24-13-25 when such law enforcement officer resides outside the county where the testimony is to be given. The claim for the witness fees shall be endorsed on the subpoena showing the dates of attendance and stating that attendance was required during the hours other than the regular duty hours to which the claimant was assigned. The claimant shall verify such statement. The dates of attendance shall be certified by the party obtaining the subpoena. The director or his or her designee shall certify that the claimant has not received any overtime pay for the law enforcement officer's attendance and that such law enforcement officer's attendance was required during hours other than regular duty hours.
    (2) Any law enforcement officer covered by paragraph (1) of this subsection who is required by subpoena to attend any court with respect to any civil proceeding, as a witness concerning any matter which is not related to the duties of such law enforcement officer, shall be compensated as provided in Code Section 24-13-25.

(d) The fee specified by subsections (b) and (c) of this Code section shall not be paid if the law enforcement officer receives any overtime pay for time spent attending such court pursuant to the subpoena.

§ 24-13-29. Legislators' exemption
No member of the General Assembly of Georgia shall be compelled to attend and give testimony at any hearing or trial or to produce evidence while the General Assembly is in regular or extraordinary session.

§ 24-13-60. Order requiring prisoner's delivery to serve as witness or criminal defendant generally; expenses; prisoner under death sentence as witness

Article 3. Securing Attendance of Prisoners

§ 24-13-60. Order requiring prisoner's delivery to serve as witness or criminal defendant generally; expenses; prisoner under death sentence as witness

(a) When a prisoner confined in any state prison, county correctional institution, or other penal institution under the jurisdiction of the Board of Corrections, other than a prisoner under a death sentence, is needed as a witness in any judicial proceeding in any court of record in this state or when it is desired that such person stand trial on an indictment or accusation charging the prisoner with commission of a felony or misdemeanor, the judge of the court wherein the proceeding is pending shall be authorized to and shall issue an ex parte order, directed to the commissioner of corrections, requiring the prisoner's delivery to the sheriff of the county where the prisoner is desired as a witness or accused. The sheriff or his or her deputies shall take custody of the prisoner on the date named in the order, safely keep the prisoner pending the proceeding, and return him or her to the original place of detention after the prisoner's discharge by the trial judge.

(b) If the prisoner was desired as a witness by this state in a criminal proceeding or if the prisoner's release to the sheriff was for the purpose of standing trial on criminal charges, the county wherein the proceeding was pending shall pay all expenses of transportation and keeping, including per diem and mileage of the sheriff, jail fees, and any other proper expense approved by the trial judge.

(c) If the prisoner was desired as a witness by the accused in a criminal proceeding or by either party to a civil proceeding, the costs and expenses referred to in subsection (b) of this Code section shall be borne by the party requesting the prisoner as a witness. The court shall require a deposit of money sufficient to defray same, except where the judge, after examining into the matter, determines that the prisoner's presence is required by the interests of justice and that the party requesting it is financially unable to make the deposit, in which case the expenses shall be taxed as costs of court.

(d) If a prisoner under a death sentence is needed as a witness for either the prosecution or the defense in any felony case, the requesting party may interview the proposed witness. Following such interview, the requesting party may move for a writ of habeas corpus ad testificandum. Such motion shall be accompanied by a proffer of the testimony of the proposed witness. The requesting party shall make such motion and proffer as soon as possible but shall not make such motion later than 20 days prior to the date of the trial. Nothing in this Code section shall limit the right of a party from presenting a material witness at a hearing or trial and to have compulsory process for that purpose.

§ 24-13-61. Issuance of order requiring prisoner's delivery to serve as witness in superior court

Any judge of the superior court may issue an order to any officer having a lawfully imprisoned person in his or her custody, requiring the production of such person before the court for the purpose of giving evidence in any criminal cause pending therein, without any formal application or writ of habeas corpus ad testificandum for that purpose.

§ 24-13-62. Issuance of writ of habeas corpus requiring prisoner's delivery to serve as witness in superior court

§ 24-13-62. Issuance of writ of habeas corpus requiring prisoner's delivery to serve as witness in superior court

The writ of habeas corpus ad testificandum may be issued by the superior court to cause the production in court of any witness under legal imprisonment.

Article 4. Uniform Act to Secure the Attendance of Witnesses from Without the State

§ 24-13-90. Short title

This article shall be known and may be cited as "The Uniform Act to Secure the Attendance of Witnesses from Without the State."

§ 24-13-91. Definitions

As used in this article, the term:

(1) "Penal institution" means a jail, prison, penitentiary, house of correction, or other place of penal detention.

(2) "State" means any state or territory of the United States and the District of Columbia.

(3) "Summons" means a subpoena, order, or other notice requiring the appearance of a witness.

(4) "Witness" means a person whose testimony is desired in any proceeding or investigation by a grand jury or in a criminal prosecution or proceeding held by the prosecution or the defense, including a person who is confined in a penal institution in any state.

§ 24-13-92. Criminal or grand jury proceeding in foreign state -- Certificate of need for testimony; expenses; punishment

(a) If a judge of a court of record in any state which by its laws has made provision for commanding persons within that state to attend and testify in this state certifies under the seal of such court that there is a criminal prosecution pending in such court or that a grand jury investigation has commenced or is about to commence, that a person within this state is a material witness in such prosecution or grand jury investigation, and that the witness's presence will be required for a specified number of days, upon presentation of such certificate to any judge of a court of record in the county in which the person is found, such judge shall fix a time and place for a hearing and shall make an order directing the witness to appear at a time and place certain for the hearing. The witness shall at all times be entitled to counsel.

(b) If at a hearing the judge determines that the witness is material and necessary, that it will not cause undue hardship to the witness to be compelled to attend and testify in the prosecution or a grand jury investigation in the other state, and the laws of the state in which the prosecution is pending or grand jury investigation has commenced or is about to commence will give to such witness protection from arrest and the service of civil and criminal process, the judge shall issue a summons, with a copy of the certificate attached, directing the witness to attend and testify in the court where the prosecution is pending or where a grand jury investigation has commenced or is about to commence at a time and place specified in the summons. In any such hearing, the certificate shall be prima-facie evidence of all the facts stated therein.

(c) If such certificate recommends that the witness be taken into immediate custody and delivered to an officer of the requesting state to assure the witness's attendance in the requesting state, such judge may, in lieu of notification of the hearing, direct that the witness be forthwith brought before him or her for the hearing; and the judge at the hearing being satisfied of the desirability of such custody and delivery, for which determination the certificate shall be prima-facie proof of such desirability, may, in lieu of issuing a subpoena or summons, order that the witness be forthwith taken into custody and delivered to an officer of the requesting state.

(d) If the witness, who is summoned as above provided, after being paid or tendered by some properly authorized person the sum of 45 cent(s) a mile for each mile by the ordinarily traveled route to and from the court where the prosecution is pending and $25.00 for each day that the witness is required to travel and attend as a witness, fails without good cause to attend and testify as directed in the summons, the witness shall be punished in the manner provided for in Code Section 24-13-26.

§ 24-13-93. Criminal or grand jury proceeding in foreign state -- Certificate of need for prisoner's testimony; order by judge in requesting state; applicability

(a) A judge of a state court of record in another state which by its laws has made provision for commanding persons confined in penal institutions within that state to attend and testify in this state may certify that there is a criminal proceeding or investigation by a grand jury or a criminal proceeding pending in the court, that a person who is confined in a penal institution in this state is a material witness in the proceeding or investigation, and that the witness's presence will be required during a specified time. Upon presentation of the certificate to any judge having jurisdiction over the person confined and upon notice to the Attorney General, the judge in this state shall fix a time and place for a hearing and shall make an order directed to the person having custody of the prisoner requiring that the prisoner be produced before him or her at the hearing.

(b) If at the hearing the judge determines that the witness is material and necessary, that the witness attending and testifying are not adverse to the interest of this state or to the health and legal rights of the witness, that the laws of the state in which the witness is required to testify will give the witness protection from arrest and the service of civil and criminal process because of any act committed prior to the witness's arrival in the state under the order, and that as a practical matter the possibility is negligible that the witness may be subject to arrest or to the service of civil or criminal process in any state through which the witness will be required to pass, the judge shall issue an order, with a copy of the certificate attached, directing the witness to attend and testify, directing the person having custody of the witness to produce the witness in the court where the criminal proceeding is pending or where the grand jury investigation is pending at a time and place specified in the order, and prescribing such conditions as the judge shall determine. The judge, in lieu of directing the person having custody of the witness to produce the witness in the requesting jurisdiction's court, may direct and require in the court's order that the requesting jurisdiction shall come to the Georgia penal institution in which the witness is confined to accept custody of the witness for physical transfer to the requesting jurisdiction; that the requesting jurisdiction shall provide proper safeguards on the witness's custody while in transit; that the requesting jurisdiction shall be liable for and shall pay all expenses incurred in producing and returning the witness, including, but not limited to, food, lodging, clothing, and medical care; and that the requesting jurisdiction shall promptly deliver the witness back to the same or another Georgia penal institution as specified by the Department of Corrections at the conclusion of his or her testimony.

(c) The order to the witness and to the person having custody of the witness shall provide for the return of the witness at the conclusion of his or her testimony, proper safeguards on his or her custody, and proper financial reimbursement or prepayment by the requesting jurisdiction of all expenses incurred in the production and return of the witness and may prescribe such other conditions as the judge thinks proper or necessary. If the judge directs and requires the requesting jurisdiction to accept custody of the witness at the Georgia penal institution in which the witness is confined and to deliver the witness back to the same or another Georgia penal institution at the conclusion of the witness's testimony, no prepayment of expenses shall be necessary. The order shall not become effective until the judge of the state requesting the witness enters an order directing compliance with the conditions prescribed.

(d) This Code section shall not apply to any person in this state confined as insane or mentally ill or under sentence of death.

§ 24-13-94. Criminal or grand jury proceeding in this state -- Issuance of certificate; how long witness detained; punishment

(a) If a person in any state which by its laws has made provision for commanding persons within its borders to attend and testify in criminal prosecutions or grand jury investigations commenced or about to commence in this state is a material witness in a prosecution pending in a court of record in this state or in a grand jury investigation which has commenced or is about to commence a judge of such court may issue a certificate under the seal of the court stating these facts and specifying the number of days the witness will be required. The certificate may include a recommendation that the witness be taken into immediate custody and delivered to an officer of this state to assure attendance in this state. This certificate shall be presented to a judge of a court of record in the county in which the witness is found.

(b) If the witness is summoned to attend and testify in this state, the witness shall be tendered the sum of 45 cent(s) a mile for each mile by the ordinarily traveled route to and from the court where the prosecution is pending and $25.00 for each day that the witness is required to travel and attend as a witness. A witness who has appeared in accordance with the provisions of the summons shall not be required to remain within this state for a longer period of time than the period mentioned in the certificate, unless otherwise ordered by the court. If such witness, after coming into this state, fails without good cause to attend and testify as directed in the summons, the witness shall be punished in the manner provided for in Code Section 24-13-26.

§ 24-13-95. Criminal or grand jury proceeding in this state -- Issuance of certificate seeking testimony of prisoner; notice to attorney general; order of compliance

(a) If a person confined in a penal institution in any other state is a material witness in a criminal proceeding pending in a court of record or in a grand jury investigation in this state, a judge of the court may certify that there is a criminal proceeding or investigation by a grand jury or a criminal proceeding pending in the court, that a person who is confined in a penal institution in the other state is a material witness in the proceeding or investigation, and that the witness's presence will be required during a specified time. The certificate shall be presented to a judge of a court of record in the other state having jurisdiction over the confined prisoner, and a notice shall be given to the attorney general of the state in which the prisoner is confined.

(b) The judge of the court in this state may enter an order directing compliance with the terms and conditions prescribed by the judge of the state in which the witness is confined.

§ 24-13-96. Exemption of witnesses from arrest and service of process

(a) If a person comes into this state in obedience to a summons directing him or her to attend and testify in this state, such person shall not while in this state pursuant to such summons be subject to arrest or the service of process, civil or criminal, in connection with matters which arose before such person's entrance into this state under the summons.

(b) If a person passes through this state while going to another state in obedience to a summons to attend and testify in that state or while returning therefrom, he or she shall not while so passing through this state be subject to arrest or the service of process, civil or criminal, in connection with matters which arose before such person's entrance into this state under the summons.

§ 24-13-97. Construction

This article shall be interpreted and construed so as to effectuate its general purpose to make uniform the laws of the states which enact it and shall be applicable only to such states as shall enact reciprocal powers to this state relative to the matter of securing attendance of witnesses as provided in this article.

5. Uniform Interstate Depositions and Discovery Act
§ 24-13-110. Short title

This article shall be known and may be cited as the "Uniform Interstate Depositions and Discovery Act."

E Depositions and Discovery Act
§ 24-13-111. Definitions

As used in this article, the term:

    (1) "Foreign jurisdiction" means a state other than this state.

    (2) "Foreign subpoena" means a subpoena issued under authority of a court of record of a foreign jurisdiction.

    (3) "Person" means an individual, corporation, business trust, estate, trust, partnership, limited liability company, association, joint venture, public corporation, government or governmental subdivision, agency, or instrumentality, or any other legal or commercial entity.

    (4) "State" means a state of the United States, the District of Columbia, Puerto Rico, the United States Virgin Islands, a federally recognized Native American tribe, or any territory or insular possession subject to the jurisdiction of the United States.

    (5) "Subpoena" means a document, however denominated, issued under authority of a court of record requiring a person to:

        (A) Attend and give testimony at a deposition;

        (B) Produce and permit inspection and copying of designated books, documents, records, electronically stored information, or tangible things in the possession, custody, or control of such person; or

        (C) Permit inspection of premises under the control of such person.

§ 24-13-112. Requirements for issuance of foreign subpoenas; application

(a) To request issuance of a subpoena under this Code section, a party shall submit a foreign subpoena to the clerk of superior court of the county in which the person receiving the subpoena resides. A request for the issuance of a subpoena under this Code section shall not constitute an appearance in the courts of this state.

(b) When a party submits a foreign subpoena to a clerk of superior court in this state, the clerk shall promptly issue and provide to the requestor a subpoena for service upon the person to which the foreign subpoena is directed.

(c) A subpoena under subsection (b) of this Code section shall:
    (1) Incorporate the terms used in the foreign subpoena; and
    (2) Contain or be accompanied by the names, addresses, and telephone numbers of all counsel of record in the proceeding to which the subpoena relates and of any party not represented by counsel.

(d) This Code section shall only apply to a subpoena to be issued in this state if the foreign jurisdiction that issued the foreign subpoena has adopted a version of the "Uniform Interstate Depositions and Discovery Act."

(e) This Code section shall not apply to criminal proceedings.

§ 24-13-113. Compelling foreign witness to appear and testify

(a) For purposes of this Code section, the term "subpoena" shall have only the meaning set forth in subparagraph (A) of paragraph (5) of Code Section 24-13-111.

(b) In addition to the mechanism for issuing subpoenas provided for in Code Section 24-13-112, whenever any mandate, writ, or commission is issued out of any court of record in a foreign jurisdiction, a witness may be compelled by subpoena issued by the clerk of superior court of the county in which such witness resides to appear and testify in the same manner and by the same process and proceeding as may be employed for the purpose of taking testimony in proceedings pending in this state.

§ 24-13-114. Service of foreign subpoena

A subpoena issued by the clerk of superior court under Code Section 24-13-112 or 24-13-113 shall be served in compliance with Code Section 24-13-23 and shall be served within a reasonable time prior to the appearance required by such subpoena.

§ 24-13-115. Applicability of Article 2 to certain provisions of this article

Article 2 of this chapter shall apply to subpoenas issued under Code Section 24-13-112 or 24-13-113.

§ 24-13-116. Protective order or enforcement, quashing, or modification of foreign subpoena

An application for a protective order or to enforce, quash, or modify a subpoena issued by the clerk of superior court under Code Section 24-13-112 or 24-13-113 shall comply with the statutes and court rules of this state and shall be submitted to the superior court of the county in which the subpoena was issued.

§ 24-13-130. When deposition to preserve testimony in criminal proceedings may be taken

Article 6. Depositions To Preserve Testimony in Criminal Proceedings

§ 24-13-130. When deposition to preserve testimony in criminal proceedings may be taken

(a)

(1) At any time after an accused has been charged with an offense against the laws of this state or an ordinance of any political subdivision or authority thereof, upon motion of the state or the accused, the court having jurisdiction to try the offense charged may, after notice to the parties, order that the testimony of a prospective material witness of a party be taken by deposition and that any designated evidence not privileged be produced at the same time and place.

(2) At any time after an accused has been charged with an offense of child molestation, aggravated child molestation, or physical or sexual abuse of a child, upon motion of the state or the accused, the court having jurisdiction to try the offense charged may, after notice to the parties, order that the testimony of any physician whose testimony is relevant to such charge be taken by deposition and that any designated evidence not privileged be produced at the same time and place.

(b) The court shall not order the taking of the witness's testimony, except as provided in paragraph (2) of subsection (a) of this Code section, unless it appears to the satisfaction of the court that the testimony of the witness is material to the proceeding and the witness:

(1) Is in imminent danger of death or great bodily harm;

(2) Has been threatened with death or great bodily harm because of the witness's status as a potential witness in a criminal trial or proceeding;

(3) Is about to leave this state, and there are reasonable grounds to believe that such witness will be unable to attend a criminal trial or proceeding;

(4) Is so sick or infirm as to afford reasonable grounds to believe that such witness will be unable to testify as a witness at a criminal trial or proceeding;

(5) Is being detained as a material witness, and there are reasonable grounds to believe that the witness will flee if released from detention; or

(6) Is 72 years of age or older.

(c) A motion to take a deposition of a material witness, or a physician as provided in paragraph (2) of subsection (a) of this Code section, shall be verified and shall state:

(1) The nature of the offense charged;

(2) The status of the criminal proceedings;

(3) The name of the witness and an address in Georgia where the witness may be contacted unless, for good cause shown, the court allows an exception to this paragraph;

(4) That the testimony of the witness is material to the proceeding or that the witness is a physician as provided in paragraph (2) of subsection (a) of this Code section; and

(5) The basis for taking the deposition as provided in subsection (b) of this Code section.

§ 24-13-131. Notice of deposition; presence of defendant at examination; child witness

(d) A motion to take a deposition shall be filed in the court having jurisdiction to try the accused for the offense charged; provided, however, that if the accused is charged with multiple offenses, only the court having jurisdiction to try the most serious charge against the accused shall have jurisdiction to hear and decide the motion to take a deposition.

(e) The party moving the court for an order pursuant to this Code section shall give not less than one day's notice of the hearing to the opposite party. A copy of the motion shall be sent to the opposing party or his or her counsel by any means which will reasonably ensure timely delivery, including transmission by facsimile or by digital or electronic means. A copy of the notice shall be attached to the motion and filed with the clerk of court.

(f) If the court is satisfied that the examination of the witness is authorized by law and necessary, the court shall enter an order setting a time period of not more than 30 days during which the deposition shall be taken.

(g) On motion of either party, the court may designate a judge who shall be available to rule on any objections to the interrogation of the witness or before whom the deposition shall be taken. The judge so designated may be a judge of any court of this state who is otherwise qualified to preside over the trial of criminal proceedings in the court having jurisdiction over the offense charged.

§ 24-13-131. Notice of deposition; presence of defendant at examination; child witness

(a) The party at whose instance a deposition is to be taken shall give to every party reasonable written notice of the time and place for taking the deposition. The notice shall state the name and address of each person to be examined.

(b) On motion of a party upon whom the notice is served, the court for cause shown may extend or shorten the time or change the place for taking the deposition.

(c) The officer having custody of an accused shall be notified of the time and place set for the examination and shall, unless the accused waives in writing the right to be present, produce the accused at the examination and keep the accused in the presence of the witness during the examination unless, after being warned by the judge that disruptive conduct will cause the accused's removal from the place where the deposition is being taken, the accused persists in conduct which would justify exclusion from that place.

(d) An accused not in custody shall have the right to be present at the examination; but failure of the accused to appear, absent good cause shown, after notice and tender of expenses, shall constitute a waiver of that right and of any objection to the taking and use of the deposition based upon that right.

(e) Notwithstanding the provisions of subsections (c) and (d) of this Code section, if the witness is a child, the court may order that the deposition be taken in accordance with Code Section 17-8-55.

§ 24-13-132. Appointment of counsel; payment of costs and expenses

(a) If an accused is financially unable to employ counsel, the court shall appoint counsel as provided in Chapter 12 of Title 17, unless the accused elects to proceed without counsel.

(b) Whenever a deposition is taken at the instance of the state, the cost of any such deposition shall be paid by the state in the same manner as any other motion hearing that may appear on the criminal calendar.

(c) Depositions taken at the instance of an accused shall be paid for by the accused; provided, however, that, whenever a deposition is taken at the instance of an accused who is eligible for the appointment of counsel as provided in Chapter 12 of Title 17, the court shall direct that the reasonable expenses for the taking of the deposition and of travel and subsistence of the accused and the accused's attorney for attendance at the examination, not to exceed the limits established pursuant to Article 2 of Chapter 7 of Title 45, be paid for out of the fine and bond forfeiture fund of the county where venue is laid.

§ 24-13-133. Manner of taking and filing deposition

Except as provided in Code Section 24-13-137, a deposition shall be taken and filed in the manner provided in civil proceedings or any nonjury motion hearing, provided that (1) in no event shall a deposition be taken of an accused party without his or her consent and (2) the scope of examination and cross-examination shall be such as would be allowed in the trial itself. On request or waiver by the accused, the court may direct that a deposition be taken on written interrogatories in the manner provided in civil proceedings. Such request shall constitute a waiver by the accused of any objection to the taking and use of the deposition based upon its being so taken. If a judge has been designated to rule on objections or to preside over the deposition, objections to interrogation of the witness shall be made to and ruled on by such judge in the same manner as at the trial of a criminal proceeding.

§ 24-13-134. Availability to state and defendant of deponent's previous statements

The state or the accused shall make available to each other, for examination and use at the taking of a deposition pursuant to this article, any statement of the witness being deposed which is in the possession of the state or the accused and which would be required to be made available if the witness were testifying at the trial.

§ 24-13-135. Admissibility and use of deposition

At the trial or upon any hearing, a part or all of a deposition, so far as otherwise admissible under the rules of evidence, may be used if the witness is unavailable. Any deposition may also be used by any party for the purpose of contradicting or impeaching the testimony of the deponent as a witness. If only a part of a deposition is offered in evidence by a party, an adverse party may require the offering of all of it which is relevant to the part offered, and any party may offer other parts. A witness is not unavailable if the exemption, refusal to testify, claim of lack of memory, inability, or absence of such witness is due to the procurement or wrongdoing of the party offering the deposition at the hearing or trial for the purpose of preventing the witness from attending or testifying.

§ 24-13-136. Objections to admission of deposition
Objections to receiving in evidence a deposition or part thereof may be made as provided in civil proceedings.

§ 24-13-137. Recordation of deposition
(a) Any party shall have the right to require that the deposition be recorded and preserved by the use of audio-visual equipment in addition to a stenographic record. The audio-visual recording shall be transmitted to the clerk of the court which ordered the deposition and shall be made available for viewing and copying only to the prosecuting attorney and accused's attorney prior to trial. An audio-visual recording made pursuant to this Code section shall not be available for inspection or copying by the public until such audio-visual recording has been admitted into evidence during a trial or hearing in the case in which such deposition is made.
(b) An audio-visual recording made pursuant to this Code section may be admissible at a trial or hearing as an alternative to the stenographic record of the deposition.
(c) A stenographic record of the deposition contemplated in this Code section shall be made pursuant to Code Section 9-11-28.

§ 24-13-138. Agreement of parties to deposition
Nothing in this article shall preclude the taking of a deposition, orally or upon written questions, or the use of a deposition by agreement of the parties with the consent of the court.

§ 24-13-139. Depositions taken only in exceptional circumstances; misuse of procedures
It is the intent of the General Assembly that depositions shall be taken in criminal proceedings only in exceptional circumstances when it is in the interests of justice that the testimony of a prospective witness be taken and preserved for use at trial. If the court finds that any party or counsel for a party is using the procedures set forth in this article for the purpose of harassment or delay, such conduct may be punished as contempt of court.

Article 7. Perpetuation of Testimony

§ 24-13-150. When proceedings to perpetuate testimony may be had
Superior courts may entertain proceedings for the perpetuation of testimony in all proceedings in which the fact to which the testimony relates cannot immediately be made the subject of investigation at law and in which, for any cause, the common-law proceeding authorized under this title is not as available, or as completely available, as a proceeding in equity.

§ 24-13-151. Inadequacy of usual proceeding to be shown
A petition for discovery merely or to perpetuate testimony shall not be sustained unless some reason is shown why the usual proceeding at law is inadequate.

§ 24-13-152. Materiality of possession of property; of availability of parties in interest

The possession of the property is immaterial; nor shall the proceeding be denied though all parties in interest cannot be ascertained or reached.

§ 24-13-153. Use of testimony

Testimony taken in the proceedings contemplated under Code Section 24-13-150 shall be used only from the
necessity of the case, but in such case may be used against all persons, whether parties to the proceeding or not.

§ 24-13-154. Costs of proceedings

The complainant shall in all cases be taxed with the costs of proceedings to perpetuate testimony.

Chapter 14. Proof Generally

Article 1. General Provisions

§ 24-14-1. On whom burden of proof lies

The burden of proof generally lies upon the party who is asserting or affirming a fact and to the existence of whose case or defense the proof of such fact is essential. If a negation or negative affirmation is essential to a party's case or defense, the proof of such negation or negative affirmation shall lie on the party so affirming it.

§ 24-14-2. Change of burden in discretion of court

What amount of evidence will change the onus or burden of proof shall be a question to be decided in each case by the sound discretion of the court.

§ 24-14-3. Amount of mental conviction required; preponderance of evidence in civil cases

Moral and reasonable certainty is all that can be expected in legal investigation. Except as provided in Code Section 51-1-29.5 or Code Section 51-12-5.1, in all civil proceedings, a preponderance of evidence shall be considered sufficient to produce mental conviction. In criminal proceedings, a greater strength of mental conviction shall be held necessary to justify a verdict of guilty.

§ 24-14-4. Determining where preponderance of evidence lies

In determining where the preponderance of evidence lies, the jury may consider all the facts and circumstances of the case, the witnesses' manner of testifying, their intelligence, their means and opportunity for knowing the facts to which they testified, the nature of the facts to which they testified, the probability or improbability of their testimony, their interest or want of interest, and their personal credibility so far as the same may legitimately appear from the trial. The jury may also consider the number of the witnesses, though the preponderance is not necessarily with the greater number.

§ 24-14-5. Reasonable doubt in criminal cases
Whether dependent upon direct or circumstantial evidence, the true question in criminal cases is not whether it is possible that the conclusion at which the evidence points may be false, but whether there is sufficient evidence to satisfy the mind and conscience beyond a reasonable doubt.

§ 24-14-6. When conviction may be had on circumstantial evidence
To warrant a conviction on circumstantial evidence, the proved facts shall not only be consistent with the hypothesis of guilt, but shall exclude every other reasonable hypothesis save that of the guilt of the accused.

§ 24-14-7. Positive testimony preferred over negative; exception
The existence of a fact testified to by one positive witness is to be believed, rather than that such fact did not exist because many other witnesses who had the same opportunity of observation swear that they did not see or know of its having existed. This rule shall not apply when two parties have equal facilities for seeing or hearing a thing and one swears that it occurred while the other swears that it did not.

§ 24-14-8. Number of witnesses required generally; exceptions; effect of corroboration
he testimony of a single witness is generally sufficient to establish a fact. However, in certain cases, including prosecutions for treason, prosecutions for perjury, and felony cases where the only witness is an accomplice, the testimony of a single witness shall not be sufficient. Nevertheless, corroborating circumstances may dispense with the necessity for the testimony of a second witness, except in prosecutions for treason.

§ 24-14-9. Inferences from evidence or lack thereof
In arriving at a verdict, the jury, from facts proved, and sometimes from the absence of counter evidence, may infer the existence of other facts reasonably and logically consequent on those proved.

Article 2. Presumptions and Estoppel

§ 24-14-20. Presumptions of law and of fact distinguished
Presumptions are either of law or of fact. Presumptions of law are conclusions and inferences which the law draws from given facts. Presumptions of fact shall be exclusively questions for the jury, to be decided by the ordinary test of human experience.

§ 24-14-21. Rebuttable presumptions of law
Certain presumptions of law, such as the presumption of innocence, in some cases the presumption of guilt, the presumption of continuance of life for seven years, the presumption of a mental state once proved to exist, and all similar presumptions, may be rebutted by proof.

§ 24-14-22. Presumption from failure to produce evidence
If a party has evidence in such party's power and within such party's reach by which he or she may repel a claim or charge against him or her but omits to produce it or if such party has more certain and satisfactory evidence in his or her power but relies on that which is of a weaker and inferior nature, a presumption arises that the charge or claim against such party is well founded; but this presumption may be rebutted.

§ 24-14-23. Presumption from failure to answer business letter
In the ordinary course of business, when good faith requires an answer, it is the duty of the party receiving a letter from another to answer within a reasonable time. Otherwise, the party shall be presumed to admit the propriety of the acts mentioned in the letter of the party's correspondent and to adopt them.

§ 24-14-24. Presumption of occupancy of railroad right of way
In any proceeding to establish a right, title, or interest in or to real property that is a part of a railroad right of way, including a right of ingress or egress, where such proceeding is based upon occupancy of the railroad right of way by a person or entity other than the railroad corporation or railroad company, there shall be a presumption that any such occupancy of the railroad right of way is with the permission of the railroad corporation or railroad company. Such presumption may be rebutted.

§ 24-14-25. Presumption of payment of check
(a) As used in this Code section:
  (1) "Bank" means any person engaged in the business of banking and includes, in addition to a commercial bank, a savings and loan association, savings bank, or credit union.
  (2) "Check" means a draft, other than a documentary draft, payable on demand and drawn on a bank, even though it is described by another term, such as "share draft" or "negotiable order of withdrawal."

(b) In any dispute concerning payment by means of a check, a duplicate of the check produced in accordance with Code Section 24-10-1003, together with the original bank statement that reflects payment of the check by the bank on which it was drawn or a duplicate thereof produced in the same manner, shall create a presumption that the check has been paid.

§ 24-14-26. Estoppels defined; enumeration generally

(a) Conclusive presumptions of law are termed estoppels; averments to the contrary of such presumptions shall not be allowed. Estoppels are not generally favored.

(b) Estoppels include presumptions in favor of:

(1) A record or judgment unreversed;

(2) The proper conduct of courts and judicial officers acting within their legitimate spheres;

(3) The proper conduct of other officers of the law after the lapse of time has rendered it dangerous to open the investigation of their acts in regard to mere formalities of the law;

(4) Ancient deeds and other instruments more than 30 years old, when they come from proper custody and possession has been held in accordance with them;

(5) Recitals in deeds, except payment of purchase money, as against a grantor, sui juris, acting in his or her own right, and his or her privies in estate, in blood, and in law;

(6) A landlord's title as against his or her tenant in possession;

(7) Solemn admissions made in judicio; or

(8) Admissions upon which other parties have acted, either to their own injury or to the benefit of the persons making the admissions.

Estoppels also include all similar cases where it would be more unjust and productive of evil to hear the truth than to forbear investigation.

§ 24-14-27. Estoppel relating to real estate

(a) Where an estoppel relates to the title to real estate, the party claiming to have been influenced by the other party's acts or declarations shall not only have been ignorant of the true title, but also ignorant of any convenient means of acquiring such knowledge.

(b) Where both parties have equal knowledge or equal means of obtaining the truth, there shall be no estoppel.

§ 24-14-28. Trustees estopped to set up title adverse to trust

Trustees and other representatives with custody of papers have ample opportunities to discover defects in the title of property in their care and shall be estopped from setting up title adverse to their trust.

§ 24-14-29. Equitable estoppel

In order for an equitable estoppel to arise, there shall generally be some intended deception in the conduct or declarations of the party to be estopped, or such gross negligence as to amount to constructive fraud, by which another has been misled to his or her injury.

Article 3. Particular Matters of Proof

§ 24-14-40. Evidence of identity; burden in civil proceedings

(a) Concordance of name alone is some evidence of identity. Residence, vocation, ownership of property, and other like facts may be proved. Reasonable certainty shall be all that is be required.

(b) In civil proceedings, parties shall generally be relieved from the onus of proving identity, as it is a fact generally more easily disproved than established.

§ 24-14-41. Proof of de facto officer

An officer de facto may be proved to be such by his or her acts, without the production of his or her commission or appointment.

§ 24-14-42. Judgment admissible; effect

A judgment shall be admissible between any parties to show the fact of the rendition thereof; between parties and privies it is conclusive as to the matter directly in issue, until reversed or set aside.

§ 24-14-43. Calendars as proof of dates

Stern's United States calendar and Stafford's office calendar shall be admissible in proof of dates for the space of time covered by them respectively without further proof.

§ 24-14-44. American Experience Mortality Tables

In all civil proceedings where the life expectancy of a person shall be an issue, the American Experience Mortality Tables shall be admissible as evidence of the life expectancy of such person.

§ 24-14-45. Other mortality tables

(a) In addition to any other lawful methods of computing the value of the life of a decedent in wrongful death cases or of determining the present value of future due earnings or amounts in proceedings involving permanent personal injuries, there shall be admissible in evidence, as competent evidence in such proceedings, either or both of the following mortality tables:

    (1) The Commissioners 1958 Standard Ordinary Mortality Table; or

    (2) Annuity Mortality Table for 1949, Ultimate.

(b) In addition to the provisions set out in subsection (a) of this Code section, the jury or court shall be authorized in cases of wrongful death or permanent personal injuries to use any table determined by the jury or court, whichever is the trier of fact, to be accurate in showing the value of annuities on single lives according to the mortality tables listed in subsection (a) of this Code section.

(c) The admissible evidence provided for in subsections (a) and (b) of this Code section shall not be the exclusive method which the jury or court is required to use in such proceedings but shall be supplementary to other lawful and allowable evidence and methods for such purpose.

§ 24-14-46. United States Department of Agriculture inspection certificates prima-facie evidence

All inspection certificates issued by the United States Department of Agriculture over the signature of any inspector thereof which are admissible in courts of the United States as prima-facie evidence of the truth of the statements therein contained shall be admissible in all courts of the State of Georgia as prima-facie evidence of the truth of the statements therein contained.

§ 24-14-47. Proof that person is dead or missing as evidence

(a) A written finding of presumed death made by officers or employees of the United States authorized to make such findings pursuant to any law of the United States or a duly certified copy of such finding shall be received in any court, office, or other place in this state as evidence of the death of the person therein found to be dead and the date, circumstances, and place of his or her disappearance.

(b) An official written report, record, or duly certified copy thereof that a person is missing, missing in action, interned in a neutral country, beleaguered, besieged, or captured by an enemy, dead or alive, made by an officer or employee of the United States authorized by any law of the United States to make the same shall be received in any court, office, or other place in this state as evidence that such person is missing, missing in action, interned in a neutral country, beleaguered, besieged, or captured by an enemy, dead or alive, as the case may be.

(c) For the purposes of subsections (a) and (b) of this Code section, any finding, report, record, or duly certified copy thereof purporting to have been signed by an officer or employee of the United States as is described in this Code section shall prima facie be deemed to have been signed and issued by such an officer or employee pursuant to law, and the person signing same shall prima facie be deemed to have acted within the scope of his or her authority.

Making and Responding to Common Objections

Professor John Barkai

> This section provides ideas about making and responding to common objections, and includes a list of common objections.

An almost endless number of objections could be made at trial. Many lists, "cheat sheets," and articles about objections can be found on the internet. This section of the book will summarize those resources, discuss the basics about objections, and provide a list of the more common objections.

Why Do Lawyers Object?
Lawyers object to:

1) limit the information fact finder can consider
   by excluding testimony, witnesses, or exhibits offered by the opposing party,

2) control the opposing lawyer's conduct
   by preventing certain questions or answers, the calling of certain witnesses, and certain statements from being made during opening statements or closing arguments,

3) preserve errors for appeal,

4) disrupt opponent's counsel's momentum,

5) send a signal to a witness,

6) communicate with the fact finder, and

7) give the witness a break and time to think.

Lawyers frequently object to the form of question (Argumentative, Ambiguous, Vague, Asked and Answered, etc.) to prevent the judge or jury from hearing inadmissible evidence. Often, however, such objections are made simply to harass, annoy, upset, or distract opposing counsel. The less experience the lawyer has, the more such objections are likely to distract. Some people consider objections made for such purposes to be "unethical;" other people consider such objections part of the competition in the adversary system. Whatever your view, be ready for such objections.

Make an Objection in Four Steps
1) Stand up.
2) Say, "Objection ____" (Fill in the blank with your reason).
3) Identify your specific objection.
    a) At a minimum, say the topic type
       (Hearsay, Relevance, Improper Impeachment, Improper Character, Lack of Foundation, Leading Question, etc.)
    b) State the evidence rule number if you know it (404, 608, etc.).
    c) A combination of the above
       ("Objection, Improper Impeachment, R613")
4) Stop talking and listen to the judge.
   Be prepared to state reasons for your objection and to make an argument to support your position.

How to Respond to an Objection
1) Speak to the judge, not the lawyer who objected.
2) Explain to the judge why your evidence should be admissible. ("Your Honor, that statement is not hearsay because I am not offering it for the truth, but rather to show notice.")
3) If you recognize that you did not lay an appropriate foundation for the evidence, explain that you will do that. ("Your Honor, I will lay the foundation.")
4) If you recognize that the opposing counsel was objecting to the form of your question, which most often happens on your direct examination, simply say, "I'll rephrase." Rephrase the question and move on with your witness examination. Do not get sidetracked by the opposing counsel who might have objected just to throw you off track.
5) For any physical piece of evidence, statement, or testimony that you will be introducing, prepare in advance and have a reason why you believe that evidence is admissible. Be ready to make that argument to the judge.
6) If the objection is to relevance, and you think you will be able to show that it is relevant after additional testimony, say to the judge, "I will connect it up in a few questions Your Honor." Such a statement is equivalent of saying "trust me." If you do say that, you had better connect it up later or else the judge will later strike your evidence and will not trust you in the future.

If You are a Judge Who Has to Rule on the Objection
1) If the specific objection was not identified, turn to the lawyer who made the objection and say, "Basis?" - Meaning, "What is the legal basis for your objection?"
2) After the lawyer has put their specific objection on the record, turn to the proponent (the lawyer who is attempting to introduce the evidence), and say, "What is your response?"
3) Allow more argument if necessary. "Counsel, how do you respond to that argument?"
4) After the arguments are completed, make your ruling.
   A) "Sustained" - meaning you agree with the objection, and you will exclude the evidence.
   B) "Overruled" - meaning you agree with the proponent of the evidence, and the evidence will be admissible.
   C) Reserve your ruling until the end of the trial. ("I will reserve my decision on this issue until the close of the testimony.")
   D) Ask lawyers to submit a written memorandum on the issue so you have a better understanding of the issue, the law, and the precedent.

Multiple Lawyers and Multiple Clients
If two or more lawyers represent one client, only one of the lawyers can object to each witness, e.g. if you do the direct, you are the only one who can object on cross. Co-counsel for the same party cannot both object or respond to objections for single witness. If there are multiple parties who each have their own lawyer, each lawyer must make their own objection to have the objections preserved for appeal.

Judges Apply the Rules of Evidence More Loosely in Nonjury Trials. Many jurisdictions seem to apply a presumption that a trial judge will ignore inadmissible evidence in a non-jury trial. Questionable evidence is very seldom basis for reversing a verdict in a nonjury trial.

The Key to Objections is Rule 103 There is a rhyme to this phrase. "Key" rhymes with "103." Rule 103 holds the key to understanding the process of objections. Read that rule very carefully. Almost all states have a rule similar to FRE 103.

FRE 103. Rulings on Evidence
(a) Preserving a Claim of Error. A party may claim error in a ruling to admit or exclude evidence only if the error affects a substantial right of the party and:
    (1) if the ruling admits evidence, a party, on the record:
        (A) timely objects or moves to strike; and
        (B) states the specific ground, unless it was apparent from the context; or
    (2) if the ruling excludes evidence, a party informs the court of its substance by an offer of proof, unless the substance was apparent from the context.
(b) Not Needing to Renew an Objection or Offer of Proof. Once the court rules definitively on the record — either before or at trial — a party need not renew an objection or offer of proof to preserve a claim of error for appeal.
(c) Court's Statement About the Ruling; Directing an Offer of Proof. The court may make any statement about the character or form of the evidence, the objection made, and the ruling. The court may direct that an offer of proof be made in question-and-answer form.
(d) Preventing the Jury from Hearing Inadmissible Evidence. To the extent practicable, the court must conduct a jury trial so that inadmissible evidence is not suggested to the jury by any means.
(e) Taking Notice of Plain Error. A court may take notice of a plain error affecting a substantial right, even if the claim of error was not properly preserved.

Important Points about Rule 103 include:
1) The objection must be timely and state the specific ground for the objection, unless it is apparent from the context.
2) If the evidence was admitted, appellate courts do not have to consider the issue unless a specific ground for the objection was timely stated.
3) If the evidence was excluded, the appellate court needs information about what the excluded evidence was going to be. That information must be provided by an "offer of proof" unless the information was apparent from the context.
4) The judge can make statements for the record about the objection, the evidence, the form of the evidence, the ruling, and can require an offer of proof in question and answer form.
5) An error is not sufficient to reverse the trial unless a "substantial right" of a party is affected.
6) Even if there was no objection at trial, "plain errors" affecting "substantial rights" can result in a reversal on appeal.

The Most Common Substantive Objections Are Based on The Rules of Evidence and Constitutional Issues. Each article within the evidence code has one or more common types of objections, such as:

	FRE
General provisions	100s
Objections	
Preliminary questions	
Limited admissibility	
Remainder of or related writings	
Judicial notice	200s
Presumptions	300s
Relevance	400s
Privileges	500s
Witnesses	600s
Competence	
Impeachment	
Opinions and expert testimony	700s
Hearsay	800s
Authentication	900s
Best evidence (original writings)	1000s

Motions in Limine

In a jury trial, a lawyer may make a pretrial motion in limine, which is a motion to exclude or admit certain evidence prior to trial. In jury trials, the motion is made outside the presence of the jury. The judge's ruling on the motion in limine can 1) prevent inadmissible evidence from being heard by a jury, or 2) allow lawyers to know that they can go forward and attempt to introduce certain evidence without risking a mistrial. Motions in limine are probably not necessary in a nonjury trial because the judge will have to hear the potentially inadmissible evidence before ruling on the motion. Therefore, even if the evidence would be ruled inadmissible, the trial judge who will be the trier of fact will have already heard the inadmissible evidence. Judges in nonjury trials are presumed to ignore inadmissible evidence.

Phrases and Questions that Suggest Inadmissible or Objectionable Information is Coming.

Lawyer: "In summary, witness you've testified that…"
Likely objection: Asked and answered

Lawyer: "Witness, what if I told you that another witness testified that…"
Likely objection: Calls for speculation, argumentative, etc.

Inadequate Objections – Not Specific Enough
"I object."
"Objection to the form of the question."
"Insufficient foundation."
"Inadmissible."
"Incompetent, irrelevant, and immaterial."

Offers of Proof are:
1) sometimes just summary statements by a lawyer of what the evidence would be if the lawyer were given an opportunity to call the witness or introduce the exhibit. ("Your Honor, if the witness would be allowed to testify, she would say that ……"), and,
2) sometimes offers of proof are questions of the lawyer and answers of the witness given in question and answer form outside the presence of the jury. (Q1 A1; Q2 A2; Q3 A3)

The Impact of Objections in Nonjury Trials – Seldom Reversed

Objections to the form of questions seldom result in reversals even in jury trials. Furthermore, it is extremely rare for an appellate court to reverse a nonjury trial decision based on an objection to the form of a question or the form of an answer. Objection battles on the forms of questions are less important in nonjury trials because the judge in a non-jury trial is presumed to ignore inadmissible evidence and decide the case only on evidence that was admissible.

Common Phrases from Court Opinions Summarizing That Inadmissible Evidence in A Nonjury Trial Will Not Result in A Reversal Include:

- "Trial judges often have access to inadmissible and highly prejudicial information and are presumed to be able to discount or disregard it."
- "In bench trials, judges routinely hear inadmissible evidence that they are presumed to ignore."
- "The presumption that the trial judge disregarded all inadmissible evidence in reaching his decision."
- "It is presumed that improper evidence taken under objection was given no weight in reaching the final conclusion [in a nonjury trial] unless the contrary appears."
- "A judge, as factfinder, is presumed to disregard inadmissible evidence and consider only competent evidence."
- "A judge "must be presumed to be able to disregard inflammatory evidence"

Common Objections to the Form of the Question

Objections to the form of the question often have no clear answers or standards. Many judges and lawyers might disagree as to whether some question is improper or not. If a rule is cited when making the objection, it would usually be Rule 611.

Argumentative (also called **Harassing, Badgering**) **(R611)**
An argumentative question asks the witness to accept the examiner's summary, inference, or conclusion rather than a fact. Often the objector is trying to protect a witness during cross-examination.
Examples of Argumentative Questions:
"Isn't what you told this judge on its face ridiculous?"
"How can you expect the judge to believe that?"
"Are you telling this court that you don't know what a machete is?"
"Do you really expect the judge to believe that?"
"Do you mean to tell me...?"
"Doesn't it seem strange that...?"
"Your kind of the hatchet man down here for the D.A.s Office, aren't you?"
"It wouldn't bother you any, to come in here and lie from the time you started to the time you stopped, would it?"

Asked and Answered: This rule is violated by repeating the same question, asked by the same lawyer, to get the same answer, from the same witness. A question which has previously been asked and answered is being asked again. The rule prevents cumulative testimony R403. Similar questions are permitted if the identical information is not repeated. This objection does not apply to prevent the same questions being asked on cross-examination that were asked on direct examination by opposing counsel. It does not prevent asking identical questions of different witnesses, nor does it prevent a lawyer representing a co-party from asking the same questions to the same witness again.

Assuming Facts Not in Evidence. This rule is violated when part of a question (usually the first part) assumes the truth of a fact that is in dispute but has not yet been proved at trial. Such a question is unfair because it cannot be answered without conceding the unproven fact. Assuming facts not in evidence may be an attempt to bring into the trial information that the lawyer is not able to prove by other means. However, questions that assume facts are permitted on cross-examination to impeach a witness's credibility.

Examples of assuming facts not in evidence:
- "When did you stop beating your wife?" (assumes previous beatings)
- "Did you know their business dropped 50% because of what the defendant did?" (assumes the defendant did the same thing)
- "How long after you purchased the items were they given to the defendant?" (assumes the purchase)

Responses:
- "I will connect it up later."(Which just means, "Judge trust me and allow a few more questions." If you request permission to "connect up later," you'd better be able to connect it up or the judge will no longer trust you.)
- "I have a good faith basis for assuming those facts. I would like to proceed without further tipping my hand."
- "This is criminal case and the defendant has a Sixth Amendment right to fully cross-examine the witness."

Beyond the Scope (of a prior direct of cross examination)

Questions on redirect examination cannot go into subject matters that have not been covered in the previous cross-examination. Similarly, questions on re-cross examination cannot go beyond the scope of redirect examination. Redirect examination is limited to issues raised by the opposing lawyer on cross-examination. If the questions go beyond the issues raised on cross, the objection will be valid.

Responses.
- "Your Honor, I'm allowed to go into this area because it goes to the witness's credibility."

Note well: Cross-examination is not limited to the subjects covered on direct examination. If it were so limited, the cross examiner would be prohibited from fully examining the witness and exposing weaknesses in the direct exam. If a "beyond the scope" objection is raised to a cross-examination question, the best response probably would be, "Your Honor, R611 allows me to cross on the subject matter of direct examination and "matters affecting the witness's credibility." My cross goes to credibility."

Compound Questions
A compound question has two or more separate questions in a single question, and usually contains the words "and" or "or." A simple "yes" or "no" answer to the question will be unclear. If the witness asked answers "yes" or "no," it is not clear if the "yes" or "no" applies to all the multiple parts of the question or just one part.
Examples:
"On that day, you went shopping <u>and</u> to the beach, didn't you?"
"Did you determine the time of death by interviewing witnesses <u>and</u> by requesting the autopsy report?"
"On Saturday, did you send the email <u>and</u> also call him?"

Cumulative (R403)
Cumulative questions ask for the same information from the same witness multiple times (like asked and answered) or ask multiple witnesses for the same information to establish the same facts.

Lack of (or insufficient) Foundation (R901)
A lack of foundation objection is proper when the lawyer asks a question before establishing the preliminary facts which would permit the questions. The evidence lacks testimony as to its authenticity or source.
Example:
"My partner saw Watkins stumble inside Cut-Rate Liquor store."
"Objection: Lack of personal knowledge – and hearsay."

Leading Question (R611)
A leading question improperly suggests the answer that the lawyer wants from the witness. Another definition is that a leading question contains the desired answer. The danger is that a leading question will make the witness agree with a false suggestion.

Often leading questions start with phrases like - "Isn't it true that… ""Did…?" or ends with "…, right?" Questions that start with the word "So" should be at least a yellow flag that the question might be leading. Although some questions are obviously leading, lawyers and judges often have different interpretations of what a leading question is. Be prepared to quickly rephrase your question if an objection to it is sustained to your question. Whether or not a question that contains the phrase "whether or not" is leading has been subject to much debate. A lawyer's nonverbal behavior or voice inflection is sometimes considered when determining whether a question is leading.

Leading is generally not permitted on direct examination. However, leading is allowed and in fact expected when cross examining a witness called by the opposing party.

Leading questions are permissible for preliminary matters, when a party calls a hostile witness or an adverse witness (FRE 611) or when a witness is very young, very old, or mentally challenged. Leading questions are also common and proper on direct examination when laying foundations because under FRE 104 the rules of evidence do not apply, except for privileges, when asking preliminary questions about the admissibility of evidence. Leading questions are also permissible when they are used like a topic sentence in a paragraph to move a witness on direct examination to another part of the scene. For example," Did there come a time when you went into the store?" Of course, the lawyer could get the same result by simply making the statement, "Now I want to ask you some questions about what you did when you went into the store." It is a common belief that the more a lawyer leads on direct examination, the less credibility the witness will have because the witness looks like they are being told what to say during the examination.

Motion to strike
Motions to strike are used two ways. First, Rule of Civil Procedure 12(f) allows for motions to strike certain pleadings. Second, Motions to strike, under evidence R103, are treated similarly to objections and ask the judge to strike inadmissible testimony from the record if the witness has just said the objectionable words. Of course, "striking" is not really striking. The inadmissible words are not removed from the court records but remain in the record even if the testimony is "stricken." The opposing lawyer can ask the judge to instruct the jury to disregard the "stricken" testimony, but psychologically, such an instruction to "disregard" the testimony might highlight the testimony for the jury. Tough choices to make.

Narrative Question, or Calls for A Narrative Answer, or simply Narrative Answer

A narrative objection can refer to a question that asks a witness to tell a story rather than to state only a few specific facts, or refer to the witness' answer which is several sentences, or even paragraphs, long. On one hand, narrative answers allow the witness to easily include inadmissible evidence, but on the other hand, a narrative story might more likely provide truthful facts.

Examples of narrative questions:
"What did you do that day?"
"Tell us about the accident."
"Now tell us what everyone said and did at that point."
"What happened that night?"
"How did the accident happen?"
Ans: "First thing I got up and I… Then I went to… After that I … She told me that… And I immediately saw the …"

Non-Responsive Answer: The non-responsive answer objection is made to an answer that does not answer the question that was asked. Simply, the witness does not answer the question asked by the lawyer. Often the witness is trying to make their own point and take control of the testimony. A problem with nonresponsive answers is that the witness is volunteering information that might be irrelevant or unfairly prejudicial. <u>In theory, only the lawyer asking the question can object to a non-responsive answer</u>. Some judges will only allow this objection from the lawyer who is asking the question. If the objection is sustained, it is often followed by a motion to strike the answer from the record. If the opposing lawyer is considering making a non-responsive answer objection, they should consider making some other appropriate objection such as "irrelevant," "unfairly prejudicial," or "lack of foundation."

Example of a non-responsive answers:
Q: "Did you see the other driver get out of his car right after the accident?"
A: "He told me he had insurance."   (non-responsive)

Q: "Weren't you the last person the victim saw on the night of his death?"
A: "I had nothing to do with that!"   (non-responsive)

Speculation – Calls for Speculation – Lack Person Knowledge. (R602)

A speculation objection is proper if the lawyer asks the witness a question that the witness has no personal knowledge about, or the witness testifies about something they have not perceived. A red flag signaling a call for speculation is often a question that starts with, Isn't it possible that…?" A better phrasing to accomplish the same objective would be to focus the question on the witness's personal knowledge and experience by asking for the same information but stating it as follows, "You don't know whether or not…, do you?"

Examples of a question calling for speculation:
"What do you think he was thinking about at that time?"
"Why would she do something like that?"

Vague and Ambiguous Question: Vague and ambiguous questions are asked in ways that are incomprehensible, incomplete, or the answer will be ambiguous. If you, as the opposing lawyer, do not understand the question asked by your opponent, then the witness probably does not understand the question either. Object.

Other Objections

Golden Rule

The Golden Rule objection is made when the opposing counsel places the trier of fact (judge or jury) in the same situation that the case is about.

Examples of a Golden Rule objection:
"Your Honor, what would you have done in a situation like that?"
"Ladies and gentlemen of the jury, would you want someone like that coming into your neighborhood?"

Speaking Objections
A speaking objection is a lawyer's attempt to influence the jury by speaking to the jury by using the objection. Although such objections are very disfavored by judges in jury trials, in nonjury trials such objections can be used to make an argument to the trial judge and influence the decision to be made on the objection.

Examples of speaking objections:
> "Well Judge, I am going to strongly object to this procedure. I feel that I am being sandbagged here and I don't appreciate it."
>
> "Your honor, it doesn't matter what the answer is. Opposing counsel just wants to make a statement. He doesn't care what this witness says."

Coaching the witness
Such objections can be used to communicate with and coach a witness.

Example of coaching the witness through an objection:
"Objection. The witness couldn't possibly know that answer."
> Witness then responds by saying, "I don't know."

Relevance
Questions in a case about some other person, some other event, and some other time, are irrelevant unless the judge find such questions to be relevant in this particular case for a special reason such as to show bias or relevant in this case under Rule 404(b). I call such irrelevant evidence <u>P.E.T. evidence</u> and tell my students that PET evidence is not admissible - evidence about some other Person, or Event, or Time. Furthermore, questions about "**what most people do**" are almost always irrelevant.

Examples of irrelevant "what most people do" objections:
> "<u>Don't most people </u>know that…?"
>
> "Don't most people speed when their car is headed downhill?"

A Few Useful Definitions

Stipulation: Agreement between opposing lawyers to admit certain evidence without the normal in-court proof. The trier of fact then assumes the fact to have been proven.

Offer of Proof: A statement by a lawyer describing evidence that the lawyer wants admitted. Proponent summarizes the substance of the excluded evidence to the judge to persuade the judge and to make a record for appeal. – R103

Motion in Limine:
A pre-trial motion seeking a ruling to admit or exclude evidence.

Limited Admissibility:
Evidence can be admitted for one purpose or against one party, but not admitted for another purpose or against another party. – R105

Intrinsic Impeachment: The impeaching statement comes out of the witness' own mouth on cross-examination. After direct exam, a witness is impeached on cross.

Extrinsic Impeachment: With extrinsic impeachment, the impeaching statement or information comes from another witness or from use of a document to impeach. If a witness is not impeached on cross by the opponent's questions (which is called intrinsic impeachment), not all types of impeachment are permitted by extrinsic impeachment. The most common limitation is FRE 608(b) prohibiting the use of extrinsic evidence of prior bad acts related to dishonestly.

Collateral Evidence: Evidence that is not relevant to the main or material issues at trial and is only relevant to a witness' credibility is called "collateral."

Collateral Matter Rule: An opposing party may not use extrinsic evidence (meaning calling another witness or using a document) to impeach a witness on a collateral matter. Bias, perception, memory, capacity and prior convictions (under R609) are always material and never collateral. Bad acts of untruthfulness under FRE 608(b) are always collateral and not admissible. Prior inconsistent statements and contradictory facts may be collateral if the impeaching facts does not relate to an outcome effecting fact and are being used only for impeaching credibility of the witness.

A List of Common Possible Objections

Ambiguous	Improper opinion
Argumentative	Improper rehabilitation
Asked and answered	Inadmissible opinion
Assumes facts not in evidence	Incompetent witness
Authentication	Incomplete Inflammatory
Badgering	Insufficient foundation
Best evidence	Irrelevant (Relevance)
Beyond the scope	Lack of foundation
Bias	Lack of personal knowledge
Bolstering	Leading question
Calls for a conclusion	Misleading
Calls for speculation	Misquotes a witness or exhibit
Chain of custody	Misquotes evidence
Collateral	Misstates witness
Competence	More prejudicial than probative
Compound question	Motion to strike
Compromise / Settlement offer	Narrative
Confrontation (lack of)	(Question calls for a narrative)
Confusing	Narrative answer
Counsel is testifying	Non-responsive
Cumulative	Nothing pending
Document speaks for itself	Outside the scope of cross
Expert (Improper opinion)	Overly broad or general
Expert (not qualified)	Parole evidence rule
Habit	Personal knowledge
Harassing the witness	Prejudice (unfair)
Hearsay	Privilege communication
Hypothetical question misused	Relevance
Improper character evidence	Speculation/ Opinion/ Lack of personal knowledge
Improper characterization	Unintelligible
Improper impeachment	Vague

There are many more possible objections,
limited only by the lawyer's imagination.

Judges and the local legal culture in your jurisdiction may have other rules or approaches to objections that are not discussed in this book. Ask around and learn about them.

Evidentiary Foundations

Foundations - Predicates - Laying the Foundation

Foundations are questions asked by a lawyer to set the groundwork (the foundation) for admitting evidence at trial. The asking of these questions is often referred to as "**laying the foundation**" for the evidence. The word "**predicates,**" when used by trial lawyers, refers to a series of form or sample questions that a lawyer must ask to establish the facts, events, or conditions which are required by the rules of evidence or caselaw before presenting other evidence. Predicates are the questions that are asked when laying the foundation for other evidence. The evidentiary foundation is like the foundation for a building. It provides a solid basis for building up the structure of the case at trial. The necessary foundational questions are not always obvious by reading the rules of evidence.

Foundations may come from local legal culture - "That's the way we do things in this jurisdiction," or from a lawyer or judge's prior experience - "That's the way I was taught to do it," or "That's what I think works best," or "That's what I am requiring you to do."

Bare-Bones Foundations

The foundations provided in this book are designed to be brief - what I call "bare-bones foundations." A "**bare-bones**" foundation uses the minimum necessary questions to admit a piece of evidence or testimony and is less concerned about the "weight" of the evidence to be admitted. Bare-bones foundations are commonly used in non-jury trials. On the other hand, what I call "**advocacy foundations**" are more common in jury trials where a jury of laypeople will make the important factual determinations in the case. An advocacy foundation uses more than the bare minimum number of questions to lay the foundation, with additional questions going to enhance the persuasiveness of the sponsoring witness and the evidence.

For example, when using a police officer's report to refresh memory, or for recorded recollection, or to impeach, the additional questions might include questions relating to the training or conduct of the officer, such as:
> "Did you have training in writing reports?"
> "How much training?"
> "When you are writing your report, you knew that your supervisor will read some of your reports?"
> "You know that your future assignments might depend on the quality of your written reports?"
> "Do you reread your report before submitting it?"
> "Do you check your report for accuracy before submitting it?"

Admissibility v. Weight

Foundations are sometimes necessary for evidence to be admissible. As such, they go to the issue of "**admissibility**," which is about "can" the evidence be included in the trial so that the trier of fact (judge or jury) can consider that evidence in decision-making. On the other hand, the "**weight**" of evidence is the "value" to be given to the piece of evidence by the trier of fact. Trial judgments are usually determined by which party's admitted evidence is more persuasive, and whether the party met the burden of persuasion to the necessary standard (such as: "preponderance of the evidence" or "beyond a reasonable doubt").

Example of Admissibility and Weight

Assume the trial is about a fight. One person says, "He hit me." The other person says, "I did not." Both statements will be admissible. But after listening to the two witnesses as well as other facts and witnesses, the trier of fact will probably assign different weights or values to the testimony of the two people. Typically, one person will be considered more credible or believable than the other person. The more reliable a person's testimony seems to the trier of fact, the more it is said to be given greater weight. It is that weight of the evidence that will eventually lead to a decision for one party or the other. A common statement made by a judge when an opposing party argues against the admissibility of testimony or other evidence is, "That goes to weight, not admissibility." Such a statement by a judge means, "You just lost your battle to exclude that evidence from the trial, but you can still argue that your case is stronger and more persuasive than your opponent's case is."

3 Simple Questions

After handing a physical item to a witness and saying for the record,

"Let me show you what has been marked as proposed exhibit number one,"

the foundation for some physical pieces of evidence can be established with as few as three questions:

> 1) Q: What is it?
>
> 2) Q: How do you know that?
>
> 3) Q: Is it in the same condition as it was on the day of …?"
>
> (Or, "Is that a fair and accurate representation of the item as it was on [a certain date]?").

Steps for Introducing Exhibits

> **Preliminary steps are:**
>
> 1) **Have the exhibit marked for identification**
> 2) **Show the proposed exhibit to opposing counsel**
> 3) **Ask permission to approach the witness with the proposed exhibit**

1. **History - How the witness knows the exhibit.**
    Offer some testimony that the witness <u>knows</u> or is <u>familiar with</u> the evidence – such as a document, physical item, photo, diagram, scene, text message, email - or recalls the statement. Even if the witness has only seen the exhibit once before or has just been to the scene shown in the photograph once before, <u>once is enough</u>.

2. **The litany (a ritualistic repetition of foundational questions)**
   a) **Ask the court clerk to mark the item** (using numbers or letters). The clerk will decide which system to use. In more serious cases in the jurisdiction's higher courts (typically where jury trials are allowed), exhibits are usually required to be marked at least before trial starts, and often during pretrial conferences.
   b) **Show opposing counsel** (this will prevent interruptions) and say, "Let the record reflect that I am showing the defense what has been marked as plaintiff's proposed exhibit number one."
   c) **Ask the judge for permission to approach the witness**. "May I approach the witness?"
   - Q: "**I show you what has been marked as** Plaintiff's (Prosecution's) (Defense's) proposed exhibit # x (or exhibit #x for identification purposes) **and ask whether you can identify it**" (You expect a "yes" answer here.)
   - Q: "**What is it?**" (They describe it in general terms. "It is the contract/photo of the scene/weapon recovered/drugs seized/diagram of the area/etc.")
   - Q: "**How do you know that?**" ("I recognize it. It has my signature on it. / I have been there many times before. / I put my initials on it and the defendant's name/etc.")

3. Show Condition or Comparison or Accuracy

Some comparison must be made between the exhibit in court and when the witness became familiar with the exhibit out-of-court. Of the examples that follow, only one such question is necessary.

- "Is this in the **same condition** as when you... [first saw it...seized it...etc.]?"
- "Is this in the **same or substantially the same condition**.... as when you…"   (for item or document)
- "Is it a **fair and accurate representation** of the X **as it was that day**?"   (for diagram or pictures)
- "**Has it changed** in any significant way?"
- "**How does it compare** to the item you saw that day?"

4. Move or Offer the Exhibit into Evidence

"Your honor, **I offer the exhibit into evidence**."

- Or, "I move the exhibit into evidence."

You could instead say, "I offer proposed exhibit # 1 into evidence as exhibit # 1," but why make it so confusing? Just say, "I offer the exhibit into evidence."

The judge <u>might</u> ask the opposing counsel, "Any objections?"

but if there is an objection to the admissibility (not the weight), the opponent should object immediately after the proponent offers the exhibit.

The judge should allow "voir dire" (immediate cross examination limited to the foundation and the admissibility) by the opponent of the exhibit.

The Common Evidentiary Foundations

(You should be able to do all of these in your sleep)

Physical Items
Photograph (printed)
Diagram of scene
Physical item seized at scene

Common Documents
Refreshing memory
Recorded recollection
Business records in paper
Business records – and self-authentication under R902
Deposition impeachment (see below)

Records and Treatises
Public record
Learned treatise –
    Use on direct supporting your expert
    Use on cross attacking their expert

Digital Evidence – from the internet, a cell phone, or a computer
    Also called - ESI – Electronically Stored Information
Emails
Text message – issues of incompleteness
Social Media - Facebook, Instagram, Twitter, Snapchat
Website posting
Voicemail recording
Videos, including on cell phone
Photo on cell phone
Fax
Chatroom conversations

Impeachment
    Impeaching by Prior Written Inconsistent statement
    Impeaching by Omission in Prior Written Statement
    Impeaching by Prior Oral Inconsistent statement
    Impeaching by Inconsistent Oral Deposition Transcript

Phrases to Move Evidence into a Trial

(Pick one and always use it)

"I offer the exhibit into evidence." (By far the easiest to use)

"Your Honor, I ask that what's been previously marked as Plaintiff's Exhibit A for Identification be admitted into evidence as Plaintiff's A." (Unnecessarily complex and you are likely to mess it up.)

"At this time, we offer Plaintiff's A for identification into evidence as Plaintiff's exhibit A."

"The Government at this time, would move to introduce Government's Exhibit No. 2 into evidence."

"Your Honor, we'd offer Defense Exhibit B into evidence."

"Your Honor, I move that Plaintiff's Exhibit 3 be introduced into evidence."

"We offer Exhibit A into evidence."

"Your Honor, I would like to submit People's exhibit 'A' into evidence."

"We would ask the Court to admit State's Exhibit 4 for Identification as State's 4."

Laying Foundations

Useful Points to Remember

Offering something "into evidence" means that in a jury trial the exhibit can go into the jury room and be reviewed as many times as the jurors want to look at it.

Make an Offer of Proof – if your evidence is not admitted. R103.

Hearsay within hearsay – statements incorporated into other statements need an additional hearsay exception to be admissible. R805 Hearsay Within Hearsay.

Public records do not have to be "open to the public" but rather are reports and records created by public (government) employees. R803(8)

A record automatically generated by a computer - is not hearsay (computer generated records). No assertion by a person.

Email offered to show notice, knowledge, or fear are not assertions and therefore not hearsay. In a contract or consent form, the words have independent legal significance, which means they operate to form a contract even if they are not true.

Demonstrative evidence – demonstrates or represents some real evidence. Also sometimes called **illustrative evidence**, as compared to **real evidence**, which as some historical connection to the case - such as being the drugs, the gun, etc.

A "**chain of custody**" **is required for fungible items** that cannot be identified and distinguished on sight, such as drugs, alcohol, and blood samples. They are as indistinguishable as grains of sand. Often, they are taken into custody and sent to a laboratory for testing. The "chain" makes sure the evidence that is tested is connected to the correct case.

Distinctive characteristics. Evidence tags with initials and case names make items unique and should qualify as a **"Distinctive characteristic"** under R901(b)(4) for authentication purposes.

The most common methods to introduce physical and documentary evidence are **using personal knowledge and distinctive characteristics.** R901(b)(1)&(4)

Affidavits are hearsay and not admissible at trial. However, affidavits can be used in summary judgment proceedings if the statements in the affidavits would be admissible in court if testified to by the declarant with personal knowledge. Therefore, lawyers should not be sign affidavits for summary judgement. Potential witnesses with personal knowledge of the facts must sign the affidavits.

HARROWing - a Barkai mnemonic/acronym formed from the first letters of evidence concepts most likely to impact admissibility decisions. Always think of HARROWing when a physical item is going to be introduced, especially if the item is a document or a physical item with words on it. **H**earsay R800s, **A**uthentication R900s, **R**elevance R401, **R**elevance R403, **O**riginal **W**ritings (Best Evidence) R1000s. HARROWing also applies to ESI (Electronically Stored Information) such as emails, texts, websites, etc.

OTP - what is the evidence "Offered to Prove?" OTP impacts relevance, admissibility, and the necessary foundation.

The rules of evidence do not tell you how to introduce exhibits although some rules do list the foundational elements which must be included in foundational questions. The hearsay exceptions of Recorded Recollection R803(5) and Records of a Regular Conducted Activity (business records) R803(6) are examples of hearsay exceptions that are so complicated that a novice trial lawyer might want to have the rule in front of them when attempting to lay the foundation.

Laying a foundation is like a sport. Practice before the game.

Steps: Mark/Pre-Mark, Show, Approach, Foundational Questions, Offer
    Mark exhibits. Have the exhibit marked before trial or prior to trial – depending on the court rules.

Magic Words: "**in the same or substantially the same condition**" or "**fair and accurate representation**," or "**fairly accurate representation**," or "**fairly represent**."

Speak in generic terms when talking about exhibits until the witness identifies the exhibit: "Proposed exhibit # 1" or "Exhibit # 1 for identification purposes," not "Your report," or "Photo of the scene."

To "publish" an exhibit means to show the exhibit to the jury or ask the judge to look at the exhibit right now, not at the end of the trial.

Chain of evidence is usually only necessary for fungible items (identical items; they all look the same), or items that need testing – drugs, alcohol, blood, DNA. Not every "kink in the link" of the chain of evidence makes evidence inadmissible. Authentication only requires production of evidence "sufficient to support a finding," R901(a)(1), which is a low standard.

Basic tasks that every trial lawyer should be able to do
- introduce documents, physical items, photographs
- refresh memory (almost always done on direct)
- use the recollection recorded hearsay exception (almost always done on direct).
- impeach (almost always done on cross); inconsistent statements & omissions.

The Best Foundation Resources
- Grimm, Joseph & Capra, Best Practices for Authenticating Digital Evidence 69 Baylor L. Rev. 1 (2017)
- Evidentiary Foundations for Government Attorneys (2015) (from National Attorneys General Training & Research Institute) - (JB: It contains many simple foundations.)
- Edward Imwinkelried, Evidentiary Foundations, (10th ed. 2018) – (The classic source for foundations, but less than you might want about ESI foundations, and more than you might want in the middle of trial.)
- Deanne Siemer, Laying Foundations and Meeting Objections (4th ed. 2013)

Important Evidence Rules to Guide You

FRE 103(c) Directing an Offer of Proof. – explains how to protect the record for appeal if your evidence is excluded at trial.

FRE 104 Preliminary questions.
(a) In General. In [deciding preliminary questions] the court is not bound by evidence rules except those on privilege.
　[**Barkai says:** that means you can lead on direct for foundations.]
(b) Relevance that Depends on a Fact. When the relevance of evidence depends on whether a fact exists, proof must be introduced sufficient to support a finding that the fact does exist.
　[**Barkai says:** that is a low threshold.]

FRE 901 Authenticating or Identifying Evidence.
(a) In General. To satisfy the requirement of authenticating or identifying an item of evidence, the proponent must produce evidence sufficient to support a finding that the item is what the proponent claims it is. [**Barkai says:** that is a low threshold]
(b) Examples. The following are examples only —
　(1) Testimony of a Witness with Knowledge. Testimony that an item is what it is claimed to be.
　(4) Distinctive Characteristics and the Like. The appearance, contents, substance, internal patterns, or other distinctive characteristics of the item, taken together with all the circumstances.
　(7) Evidence About Public Records.
　(9) Evidence About a Process or System.

FRE 612 Writing Used to Refresh a Witness's Memory. Witness does not need to be the author. Anything can be used to refresh memory - even "my left shoe," which is my in-class example.

FRE 613 Witness's Prior Statement. Impeachment by inconsistent statements and omissions.

FRE 801(d)(1) Not Hearsay: A Declarant-Witness's Prior Statement. (Inconsistent under oath, consistent, or prior ID)

FRE 803(6) Records of a Regularly Conducted Activity
(JB: business records are **KRAP**)
　(**K**ept in the course, **R**egular practice, **A**t or near the time, **P**ersonal knowledge)

FRE 902 Evidence That Is Self-Authenticating

902(11) Certified Domestic Records of a Regularly Conducted Activity. [Note: There are many certification forms available on the internet. At least 32 states have adopted this 2002 FRE amendment.]

902(13) Certified Records Generated by an Electronic Process or System. [Only 11 states have adopted this 2017 FRE amendment.]

902(14) Certified Data Copied from an Electronic Device, Storage Medium, or File. [Only11 states have adopted this 2017 FRE amendment.]

R105 Limited Admissibility (admitted against only one party or for a limited purpose)
Only 3 states and the District of Columbia have no rule or statute similar to R105 and rely on case law (Massachusetts, Missouri, and New York).

R106 Remainder of / related writing [Barkai says this means to admit the remainder now]. Only 4 states have no rule or statute (Kansas, Massachusetts, Missouri, and New York).

R1006 Summaries…voluminous writings which cannot conveniently be examined in court.

The Opponent Has the Burden
On the Issue of Trustworthiness of Records

Since this 2014 FRE amendment, the burden of showing a record lacks trustworthiness is on the opponent in the Federal rules – FRE 803(6)(7)(8) …"and, the opponent does not show …a lack of trustworthiness."

> 8 states have also amended their rules placing the burden of showing that the source of the source of information or other circumstances indicate a lack of trustworthiness on the opponent (Arizona, Mississippi, New Hampshire, New Mexico, Oregon, South Dakota, Utah, and West Virginia).

Basic Foundations & Impeachment Examples

Several of the following foundation and impeachment examples are based upon the facts of

NITA Liquor Commission v. Cut-Rate Liquor and Jones*

In this famous, fictional case from NITA (National Institute of Trial Advocacy), Walter Watkins was observed going into the Cut-Rate Liquor Store by Officer Bier and his partner from their unmarked car which was parked across the street from the liquor store. The officers had a partial view into the store and saw Watkins appear to purchase liquor at the counter. Watkins was arrested outside the store as he was leaving with a brown paper bag which contained a bottle of Thunderbird Wine. Cut-Rate Liquors and the clerk Dan Jones were issued citations for selling liquor to a person under the influence of liquor.

* This NITA Liquor Problem is used with the permission of the National Institute of Trial Advocacy (NITA). The terms "Officer Bier, Thunderbird Wine, Jackson & 7th Street, April 5th, Walter Watkins, and shoulders up" used in this publication are original to the Nita Liquor Commission v. Cut-Rate Liquor and Jones problem from *Problems in Trial Advocacy* by Donald H. Beskind and Anthony J. Bocchino, published by the National Institute of Trial Advocacy. The basis of the NITA Liquor problem and the specified terms are used here with permission.

NITA Liquor Commission
v.
Jones

The Facts

This case is a civil action brought by the Liquor Commission against Dan Jones and the Cut-Rate Liquor Store for civil penalties, including possible revocation of Cut-Rate's liquor license. Investigator Bier is a typical investigator-police officer and has investigated many such incidents. Bier's official report appears on the next page along with a diagram of the scene.

Dan Jones and the Cut-Rate Liquor Store deny that Watkins was intoxicated on the evening of April 5 when he was in their store. Jones says that Watkins did not appear to be intoxicated when he observed Watkins in the store. Watkins was convicted of public intoxication at a prior trial. Watkins is not present for this Cut-Rate case.

1. Prepare to do a direct examination of Officer Bier for the government.

2. Prepare to do a cross examination of Officer Bier for the Defense.

Officer Bier's Report

NITA LIQUOR COMMISSION OFFICIAL REPORT

My partner Donald Smith and I are investigators for the Nita Liquor Commission. On the evening of April 5, at approximately 8:45 p.m., we were parked near the Cut-Rate Liquor Store when we observed an individual, later identified as Walter Watkins, attempting to cross 7th Street. Mr. Watkins was staggering and had great difficulty making it to the other side of the street. He stumbled and almost fell at the curb on the south side of 7th Street. He walked to the entrance of the Cut-Rate Liquor Store, and then paused for a few moments before he entered the store. The front of the store had a plate glass window with displays and advertising in it. From our car, we could see Mr. Watkins from the shoulders up through the window. We observed Mr. Watkins approach the counter and say a few words to the clerk, Dan Jones. A few minutes later, Watkins emerged from the store carrying a bottle of Thunderbird wine in a brown paper sack.

I stopped Mr. Watkins as he exited the store. I detected the odor of alcohol and administered a field sobriety test. I then arrested Watkins and issued him a citation for public intoxication, seized the wine, and issued a citation to Dan Jones and the Cut-Rate Liquor store for violation of H.R.S. 281-78 which contains the following language:

> No licensee nor its employees shall sell or furnish any liquor to any person at the time under the influence of liquor.

I have attached a diagram of the scene to this report.

Date: April 5   Time: 22:15

                                    signed J. Bier
                                    _____

Diagram of Cut-Rate Liquor Store Area

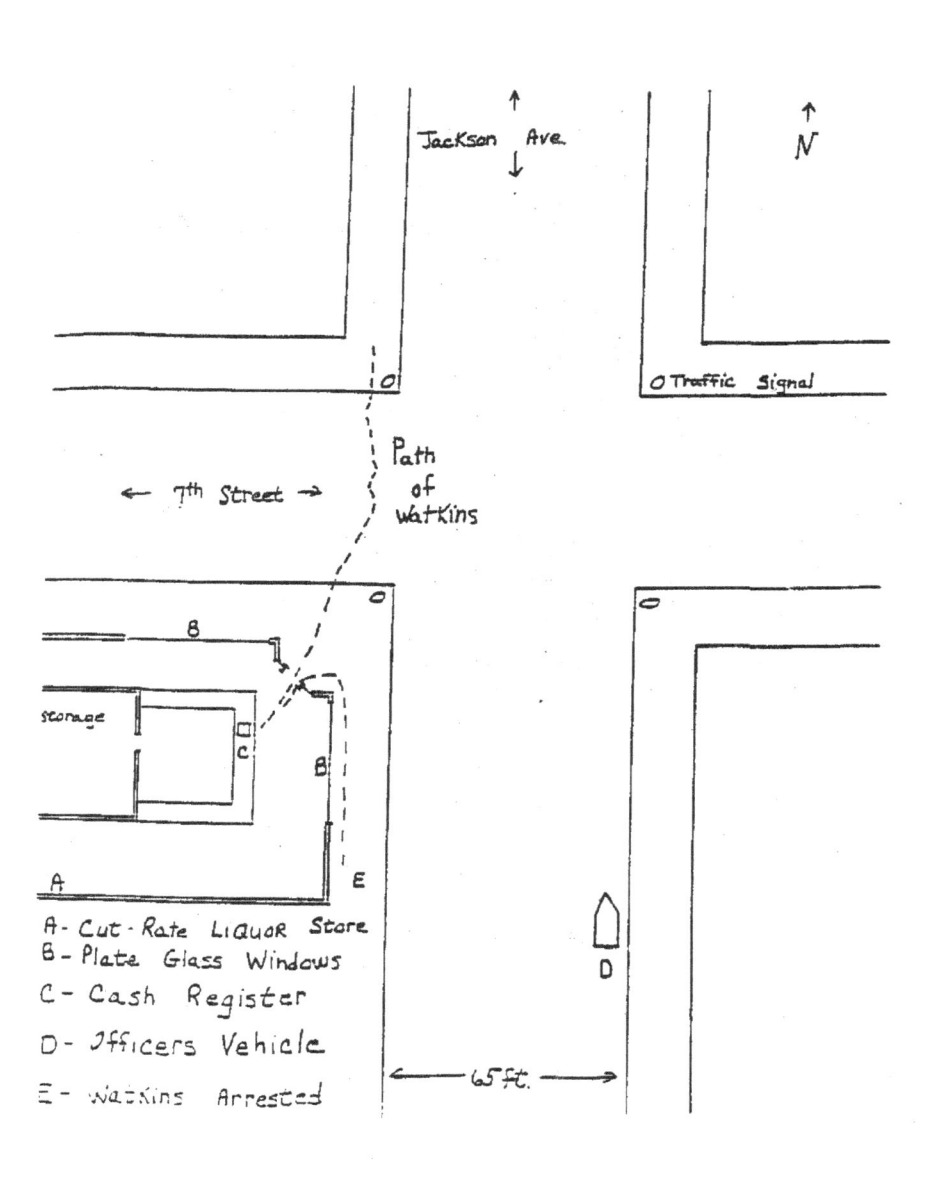

Jackson Ave.

N

○ Traffic Signal

← 7th Street →

Path of Watkins

B

storage

C

B

A   E

A - Cut-Rate Liquor Store
B - Plate Glass Windows
C - Cash Register
D - Officers Vehicle
E - Watkins Arrested

D

← 65 ft. →

Photograph of a Scene

Introduce a photograph of Cut-Rate Liquor Store where the clerk and the liquor store were charged with selling liquor to an intoxicated person. R901(B)(1) (Testimony of a Witness with Knowledge)

Q: Officer Bier, where were you on the night of April 5?
A: Parked in an unmark car outside Cut-Rate Liquor Store.

Q: Let me show you what has been marked as Plaintiff's proposed exhibit # 1. <u>What is it?</u>
A: It is a photograph of Cut-Rate Liquor Store where I was parked on April 5$^{th.}$

Q: <u>How do you know that?</u>
A: I was at the store that night. I recognize it. I took the photo.

Q: Is the photograph a <u>fair and accurate representation</u> of Cut-Rate Liquor store as it appeared <u>on April 5th</u>?
A: Yes.

Q: Your Honor, I offer the exhibit into evidence.

Enhancements/Additional Questions
- "Please describe the appearance of the store."
- "How many times have you seen the Cut-Rate Liquor Store?" (Ask this question only if the witness has been to the store many times. However, being there once is enough for the foundation.) The witness can authenticate the photo even if the trial event was the only time the witness ever saw the store pictured in the photo

Additional Points:
- The photographer is not a necessary witness.
- The witness's personal knowledge of the contents of the photograph is all that is necessary.
- The witness does not have to have seen the photograph before coming to court.
- Print the photo and bring copies to court for the judge, jury, and opposing counsel.
- The photo could be a "Street view" from Google Maps that the witness has never seen before.

Diagram of the Scene

Demonstrative Evidence

Diagram from Officer Bier's Report

After some testimony about the events.

Q: Officer Bier, did you make a diagram of the scene that night? (Ans: Yes)

Q: Let me show you what has been marked as Plaintiff's proposed exhibit # 1. <u>What is it?</u> (Ans: My diagram)

Q: <u>How do you know that?</u> (Ans: I drew it. I remember it. That's my writing)

Q: Is it a <u>fair and accurate representation</u> of the intersection of Jackson and 7th Streets <u>on April 5th</u>? (Ans: Yes.)

Q: Is the proposed exhibit in the <u>same condition</u> as it was when you drew it on April 5th? (Ans: Yes.)

Q: Your Honor, I offer the exhibit into evidence.

Real Evidence

The Bottle of Thunderbird Wine Seized by Officer Bier

After some testimony about the events.

Q: Officer Bier, <u>what, if anything, did you recover</u> from Mr. Watkins that night?
(Ans: A bottle and a bag)

Q: Let me hand you what has been marked as Plaintiff's proposed exhibit # 2. <u>What is it?</u>
(Ans: The bottle and bag I seized from Watkins)

[If the bottle is in a bag, leave it in the bag. Have both the bottle and bag marked separately, e.g., Exhibits 1 and 2, A and B, 1 and 1A. Let the witness take the bottle out of the bag, like unwrapping a present. It will create some interest in what might be an otherwise boring trial.]

Q: <u>How do you know that?</u>
[Ans: My initials, in my handwriting, are on the bag along with the words "Cut-Rate Liquor" and "April 5."]

Q: Is the proposed exhibit # 2 <u>in the same or substantially the same condition</u> as it was when you recovered it from Watkins on April 5th?
(Ans: Generally, yes. However, some of the liquid was removed for testing for alcohol.)

Q: Your Honor, I offer the exhibit into evidence.

Offering A Contract into Evidence

Q: Mr. Johnny, I now want to ask you some questions about your dealings with Mr. King. In September, two years ago, did you have several conversations with Mr. King?
A: Yes. I did.

Q: What was the result of those conversations?
A: Mr. King and I entered into a contract for legal work.

Assume the exhibit has been pre-<u>marked</u> before the day of trial

Q: Let the record reflect that I am <u>handing</u> Mr. Johnny what has been pre-marked, as required by Court Rule, Plaintiff's proposed Exhibit # 1.
<u>What is it Mr. Johnny?</u>
A: It's the contract between me and Mr. King for the legal work that I was going to do for him.

Q: <u>How do you know that?</u> [Prepare the witness to answer this question]
A: I drafted this contract. I recognize it. That's my signature on it as well as Mr. King's.

Q: Is the contract in the <u>same condition</u> as it was two years when you both signed it.
A: Yes. There are no alterations to the contract.

Q: You Honor, I <u>offer</u> the exhibit into evidence

Laying Foundations

Refreshing Memory
(Anything can be used to refresh memory)

<u>Refreshing memory is almost always done on direct examination.
Impeachment is almost always done on cross examination.</u>

In the NITA case, assume witness Bier forgets some of Mr. Watkin's movements on the street. Refresh Bier's memory from his report. R612.

Q: Please describe Watkin's movements as he crossed 7th Street.
A: He staggered and had great difficulty getting to the other side of the street.

Q: Do you recall anything else about Watkins as he crossed the street.
A: Not really

Q: Officer Bier <u>did you make a report</u> in this case? A: Yes.

Q: Let me hand you what has been marked as Plaintiff's proposed exhibit # 3. <u>What is it?</u>
[Note: You are not going to introduce the document. Some judges might allow you to refresh memory without marking the exhibit, but the better practice is to have the document marked.]
A: My report.

Q: Please <u>read it to yourself</u>, especially the 4th and 5th lines.
   (Note: You can focus the witness on what you want to witness to pay attention to.)

Q: <u>Let the record reflect that I am taking proposed exhibit # 3 away</u> from the Officer.
Now Officer Bier, is your memory refreshed?
A: Yes.

Q: What else do you now recall about how Watkins crossed 7th Street?
A: Watkins stumbled as he crossed 7th Street
   (Discussion continued on the next page)

Recommendation: I suggest that you do not ask the witness, "Would anything refresh your memory." Just start refreshing. Isn't it strange to say, "Witness, I know you cannot remember, but can you remember anything that would help you remember what you have already forgotten?" Just refresh.

Additional points: The document used to refresh is not introduced into evidence. The witness' memory was refreshed. There is no need to introduce the document. There is no hearsay issue.

Writing Used to Refresh Memory

If a writing was used to refresh memory, R612 allows

>as a matter of right, if the document was used in court;
>with judge's discretion, if the document was used out of court

the opponent to:

1) see the writing in court,
2) inspect it
3) cross-examine on it, and
4) introduce portions of it (related to the testimony)

Simply: **Get (produced), Inspect, Cross, Introduce.**

However, it would be very unusual for an opponent to introduce the document because most of the document would hurt the opponent's case. If the opponent wanted to introduce only portions of the document, the lawyer who used it to refresh memory would have an argument that under R106, in fairness other parts of the document should be considered at the same time.

Rule 612. Writing used to refresh memory. (paraphrased)
   If a witness uses a writing to refresh memory for the purpose of testifying, either:
   (1) while testifying; or
   (2) before testifying, if the court in its discretion determines it is necessary in the interests of justice,
      an adverse party is entitled
      to have the writing produced at the hearing,
      to inspect it,
      to cross-examine the witness thereon, and
      to introduce in evidence those portions which relate to the
         testimony of the witness.

Refreshing Memory with a Leading Question

(Using the same facts as the previous example)

Q: Do you recall anything else about Watkins as he crossed the street.
A: Not really

Q: Did he stumble and almost fall?

Opposing Lawyer: Objection: Leading

Q: I'll rephrase my question. What else do you recall about Watkins as he crossed the street.
A: Now I recall that he did stumble and almost fell crossing the street. I'm nervous. I forgot.

Note: The witness's credibility might have decreased somewhat because of the leading question, but the lawyer got the answer that was needed. The less important the information, the more likely leading will have little or no impact on your case.

Leading on Minor Issues When the Witness Has Gone Off Course

Q: What day of the week did this happen?
A: Tuesday.

Q: You said Tuesday. Did you actually mean Monday?
A: Oh right, sorry. It was Monday.

Recorded Recollection (Author's Rule)

Recorded recollection is a hearsay exception that allows <u>for reading into evidence</u> a statement that was made by a witness on the stand who can no longer recall the facts even after there has been attempts to refresh the witness's memory. Recorded recollection is <u>almost always done on direct examination</u> with a witness the lawyer has called to testify. This foundation is complicated and not intuitive.

In the NITA problem, assume that attempts to refresh the witness's memory did not work. Therefore, assume the previous question and answer were:

Q: What else do you now recall?
A: Sorry, I truly do not remember any more.

[Lawyer now moves into the foundation for Recorded Recollection, under R803(5).

Q: Let me again show you proposed exhibit # 3. That is your report of this incident, right? (Note: Leading is appropriate when establishing any foundations under FRE 104(a) and similar state rules).
A: Yes

Q: You made that report when the incident was <u>fresh</u> in your mind?
A: Yes, just about an hour after the incident.

Q: Does the report <u>accurately reflect your knowledge</u> of the incident at the time of the incident?
A: Yes.

Q: Although you <u>once knew the details</u> of the incident and wrote them in your report, right now <u>you cannot now recall</u> the details of the incident well enough <u>to testify fully and accurately</u>, right?
A: Yes.

Q: Your honor, I would now <u>like to read</u> into the record those parts of the report that the witness no longer remembers. [Or, you could ask to have the witness read the portions of the report.]

(Discussion continued on the next page)

FRE 803(5) Recorded Recollection A record that:
(A) is on a matter the witness once knew about but now cannot recall well enough to testify fully and accurately;
(B) was made or adopted by the witness when the matter was fresh in the witness's memory; and
(C) accurately reflects the witness's knowledge.
If admitted, the record may be read into evidence but may be received as an exhibit only if offered by an adverse party.

Additional Points: "Admission" into evidence comes from reading parts of the document into evidence. The document is <u>not physically admitted</u> by the proponent of the evidence. It cannot be taken into the jury room. Information in this hearsay document is admitted (heard) only once like oral testimony. Also, admitting information from a "Learned Treatise" under that hearsay exception R803(18) is a similar process in that the information from the treatise can only be read and not physically introduced.

Almost always, the witness was the author of the document used as the recorded recollection. Refreshing memory under R612 and recorded recollection are almost always done on direct examination. Witnesses are impeached on cross, not refreshed. You would not normally use recorded recollection on cross because almost all of the document goes against your client.

I think <u>most lawyers prefer to read the recollection on direct examination themselves</u> and not have the witness read it. By reading the recollection yourself, you can add what you consider the best tone, volume, pace, and emphasis for your case. Remember, when you use a past recollection recorded with your witness on direct, you cannot physically introduce the document into evidence. The proponent of the past recollection recorded "admits" the recollection by reading it, not physically admitting it.

<u>Recorded recollection documents are not business records. Business records do get admitted into evidence</u>. The difference is that if admitted, the evidence can be taken into the jury room and be consulted by the jury many times during deliberations.

A past recollection recorded includes all notes that a witness makes on any type of document. In evidence class, I pull out my wallet and show students all the recorded recollections that I have in my wallet (post-it notes, notes on business cards, notes on little scraps of paper, etc.) and any notes I have taken on my cell phone. Recorded Recollections and Statements in Learned Treatises under R803(18) are two types of hearsay documents which can only be read into evidence but not physically introduced, at least not by the proponent of a recorded recollection.

Business Records - Custodian of Records
(The actual hearsay exception is for "Regularly Conducted Activity," but is usually called "Business Records")

To prove that Cut-Rate Liquors had Thunderbird Wine in stock on April 5, a business record can be offered.

Q: Please state your name, occupation, and why you are here today.
A: I am Mr. Data, an employee of Cut-Rate Liquors. My duties at Cut-Rate include serving as the custodian of business inventory records for Cut-Rate. I am here today pursuant to a subpoena to bring inventory records of Cut-Rate for April 5th.

Q: Did you bring with you today a copy of the Cut-Rate inventory records pertaining to Thunderbird wine for April 5th with you?
A: Yes.

Q: Do you know how Cut-Rate maintains its inventory records?
A: Yes.

Q: I show you what has been pre-marked as proposed exhibit # 1 and ask if you can identify what it is?
A: Yes, I can. Those are the Cute-Rate inventory records that I brought to court.

Q: Are those inventory records made by a person with personal knowledge, at or near the time the inventory is taken?
A: Yes.

Q: Are those records kept in the course of a regularly conducted activity of a business?
A: Yes.

Q: Is making those records a regular practice of Cut-Rate's business?
A: Yes.

Q: Your Honor, I offer the exhibit into evidence.

Publishing a Business Record: After being admitted, the business record can be "published" (which means it can be shown to the trier to fact). Depending on the judge's practice, the lawyer might be able to have the information from the record read to jury when it is admitted. If so, the Q & A could be:

Q: What do those records say about whether Cut-Rate had Thunderbird Wine in stock on April 5th?
A: "Thunderbird Wine, quantity 5," which means that Cut-Rate had five bottles of Thunderbird Wine in stock on April 5.

Remember, **business records are KRAP**. That acronym always gets my students' attention, and it helps them remember the foundation's components. **KRAP** – means:
Kept in the course,
Regular practice,
At or near the time,
Personal knowledge

The **custodian of records or other qualified witness** required by the business record evidence rule is often the owner of the business, a bookkeeper, or anybody who works in the business. They just have to be able to answer questions to provide the appropriate foundation.

Although it adds to the weight of the evidence to have a witness who has been employed for many years in the data collection of the business, that is not required. The custodian only needs to be able to testify to the foundation requirements. The custodian could have only been the custodian for one day, if they can credibly answer the foundational questions (although that fact might go to the weight of the evidence, but not its admissibility). The custodian does not have to be employed on the day the record was made.

I would prefer to use a self-authenticating business record. The custodian is open to a difficult cross.
"Do you know who made the business entry?" – Know their work history? Have they been disciplined? Know their accuracy? Are they still with the company? (Of course, you need a good faith basis to ask such cross questions).

Laying Foundations

Self-Authenticating Business Records

The Federal Rules of Evidence were amended in 2002 to allow business records to be self-authenticated by a written certification of the custodian or other qualified witness, which means that a witness does not have to appear in court. FRE 902(11)(12). Many states have created statutes or forms to be used for the certification. An example of such a certification affidavit follows and many are available on the internet.

> 32 states have rules on self-authenticating business records (records of regularly conducted activity)

Texas Form – A Sample

	Business Records Affidavit	
FORM AR-1(08/10)	Tax Year	HCAD Account Number

This affidavit should be executed before a Notary Public or other official authorized to administer oaths and attached to the applicable business records. Please print or type.

Before me, the undersigned authority, personally appeared _____ who being by me duly sworn, deposed as follows:

My name is _____. I am of sound mind, capable of making this affidavit, and personally acquainted with the facts herein stated.

I am the custodian of the records of _____ Attached hereto are
(NAME OF BUSINESS)
_____ pages of records from _____ These
(NAME OF BUSINESS)
said _____ pages of records are kept by _____
(NAME OF BUSINESS)
in the regular course of business, and it was the regular practice of said entity for an employee or representative with knowledge of the act, event, condition, opinion, or diagnosis, recorded to make the record or to transmit information thereof to be included in such record, and the record was made at or near the time or reasonably soon thereafter. The records attached hereto are the original or exact duplicates of the original.

_____
Affiant's Signature

SWORN TO AND SUBSCRIBED before me on the _____ day of _____

_____
Notary Public, State of Texas

(seal)   _____
Notary's Printed Name

_____
My commission expires

Demonstrative Evidence Similar to the Real Item

Assume the bottle of Thunderbird wine in the Nita Liquor Commission case was dropped and broken after the contents had been tested in the lab and showed that it contained alcohol. At trial, a lawyer wants to introduce a bottle similar to the actual bottle of Thunderbird wine.

Q: Officer Bier, do you recognize proposed exhibit # 5?
A: Yes. I do.

Q: What is it?
A: It is a bottle like the one sold by Cut-Rate on the night of the incident.

Q: How do you know that?
A: I am a Liquor Commission Investigator. I am very familiar with Thunderbird wine as part of my job.

Q: "Is this bottle similar to the bottle you seized from Watkins on April 5?"
A: Yes.

Q: I offer the exhibit into evidence.

If there is a relevance objection to the "similar" bottle, the lawyer examining the witness needs to be ready to say, "Your honor, this bottle is relevant to show ... [some appropriate statement]." For example, the size and weight of the bottle suggests that Mr. Watkins could not have smuggled the bottle into the liquor store under his clothing. The similar bottle is not offered as the bottle that was sold that night, but it is being offered to prove something else, which is an example of limited admissibility under R105. The lawyer should not say, although it might be true, "My evidence professor always told us to introduce some physical evidence into the trial to wake up the trier of fact." [Such a statement offers a good trial strategy, but not a good response to the judge's question about relevance.]

Laying Foundations

Impeachment by Prior Written Inconsistent Statement
FRE 613

Impeach Officer Bier from his report in the NITA problem, assuming Bier testified on direct exam, "I saw Watkins from the waist up inside the store."

> Direct exam testimony was "...from the <u>waist</u> up...."
> Report says "...from the <u>shoulders</u> up..."

Q: T<u>oday</u> you testified on direct examination[1] that you could see Watkins inside the store from the <u>waist up</u>? (said in a disbelieving tone) (Commit to today's testimony.)
A: Yes.

Q: You made a written report in this case within a few hours of the incident? (Credit prior statement's reliability)
A: Yes.

Q: Let the record reflect that I am handing the witness proposed exhibit #x. Mr. Bier, proposed exhibit #x is the report you made within a couple of hours after the incident?
A: Yes.

Q: That is your signature on the report?
A: Yes

Q: Even though you said on direct examination that you could see Mr. Watkins inside the store from the waist up, doesn't it say right here in your report (pointing to it) that "we could see Mr. Watkins from the <u>shoulders up</u> through the window"?
A: Yes.

(Discussion continued on the next page)

---

[1] I suggest that you only use the phrase – "You testified on direct" – when you are going to impeach a witness with a prior statement. Do not use that phrase when you are asking questions about a real event that took place in your case. What happened on the day of the incident might be different than what a witness testified to on direct. You should keep the trier of fact's attention on the incident itself, not the testimony on direct – unless you are impeaching that direct testimony.

Stop. Ask no further questions on this topic. Don't say, "Are you lying today or were you lying then?" Such a question is probably argumentative and objectionable anyway. Do not argue with the witness or ask the witness to admit they are not telling the truth. Save the credibility argument for closing argument. In closing argument, you can make an argument without having the witness trying to explain away your impeachment.

Understand the difference between testimony about "waist up" and "shoulders up." If Officer Bier could see Mr. Watkins inside the store from the waist up, he could have seen the bottle of wine, the cash register, any money changing hands, and the wine bottle changing hands. All those facts go to showing that there was a sale of wine in violation of the statute. However, if the officer could only see inside the store at the shoulders up level, then he was not able to see any direct sale and the defense has a better argument.

Three impeaching steps here: commit; credit; and confront. 1) <u>Commit</u> the witness to the statement made on direct, 2) <u>credit</u> the prior out-of-court statement, and 3) <u>confront</u> the witness with the difference.

<u>By putting the conflicting statements in one sentence by using a dependent clause</u> ("Even though you said on direct examination that…"), <u>the trier of fact cannot miss the contradiction.</u> Some impeaching lawyers will emphasize certain words in their questions, so the trier of fact does not miss the inconsistency. For example, they would emphasize with tone, volume, pace, and any other nonverbal's, the words "waist up" and "shoulder up." The impeaching lawyer might want to make eye contact with the judge or the jury when emphasizing those words.

Additional questions that are sometimes asked, especially if it is a jury trial:
    Your prior statement was made closer in time to the event than your statement today?
    Your memory was better at the earlier time?
    You have had training on how to write reports?
    You know that your supervisor will read your reports?
    You know that you are evaluated on, and perhaps even promoted or demoted based on the quality of your reports?

Impeachment by Omission

Assume that <u>Bier testified on direct exam</u>, "As I was sitting in my car watching Watkins <u>inside the store, I saw that Watkins stumble and almost fall as he approached the counter</u>." However, Officer Bier's report does not say that Watkins stumbled and almost fell inside the store. In fact, the report indicates that the officer could only see Watkins from the shoulders up as he approached the counter. Impeachment by omission - meaning that the witness testified in court to something that was not in the report - it is a little harder to accomplish than a direct prior inconsistent statement, but it is still very doable.

Q: <u>You testified on direct</u> examination that you saw Mr. Watkins stumble and almost fall as he approached the counter inside from the store? (Credit prior statement's reliability)
A: Yes.

Q: You made a written report in this case within an hour of the incident, right?
A: Yes.

Q: I am handing the witness proposed exhibit #x.
This is the report you made within a couple of hours after the incident, isn't it?
A: Yes.

Q: That is your signature on the report, isn't that true?
A: Yes

Q: <u>Even though you said on direct examination</u> that you saw Mr. Watkins <u>stumble and almost fall</u> as he approached the counter <u>inside</u> the store, <u>nowhere</u> in this report that you prepared <u>does it state</u> that you saw Watkins stumble and almost fall <u>inside</u> the store, does it? [If the witness takes time to look for it in the report, give them as much time as they want to take.
A: No, it doesn't say that.

The report says nothing about Watkins' behavior in the store. Behavior in the store is critical to proving that defendant Jones knew that Watkins was intoxicated.

Additional questions beyond the bare-bones foundation.
   Lawyer could build up the report, for example:

>   "You try to put everything that is important in the report, right?"
>   "They taught you to do that in the department training, right?"

The potential re-direct examination:
If it were my witness who was impeached, my redirect would go something like this:
   Q: Officer, how do you explain what seems to be an inconsistency between your direct testimony that Watkins stumbled inside the store and your report, which does not mention Watkins stumbled inside the store?
   A: [Perhaps the best answer would be] I can't put everything into the report. But I clearly remember that he stumbled inside the store.

Impeachment by Inconsistent Oral Deposition

Assume the same factual inconsistency of testimony on direct examination that Mr. Watkins stumbled inside the store, but this time also assume that Officer Bier gave an oral deposition under oath and gave an answer that did not mention any stumbling inside the store.

After laying a foundation which would include the procedures involved in the deposition, such as:
- You came to my office?
- You took an oath to tell the truth?
- I told you that if you didn't understand the question, you should tell me you don't understand?
- You had an opportunity to review and correct the transcript some weeks after the deposition?
- After you read the typed deposition, you signed the deposition as being accurate?

then complete the impeachment by reading the questions that were asked and the answers that were given at the deposition.

The impeaching sequence could go something like this:

Q: Even though you said on direct that Watkins stumbled and almost fell in the store when he was at the counter, at your deposition weren't you asked this question, and didn't you give this answer:

> Q: Now Officer Bier, how was Watkins walking when he was inside the store?
> A: I can't say for sure. My view into the store was obstructed.

A: Yes, that is what it says.

You want to confine your questions to what the witness said at the deposition, not what the witness remembers now. Your opponent will no doubt do redirect examination to try to rehabilitate the witness.

Impeachment by Inconsistent Oral Deposition - Short Form

On direct examination, the witness said, "The light was <u>green</u>."

You want to impeach with the witness' deposition that says, "The light was <u>red</u>."

Q: On direct examination you said the light was green?
A: Yes.

Q: Even though on direct examination you said that the light was green, at the deposition weren't you asked the following question, and didn't you give the following answer?
Q: What color was the light?
A: The light was red.
A: Yes.

Impeachment by Inconsistent Oral Deposition - Long Form

On direct examination, the witness said, "The light was green."
You want to impeach with the witness' deposition that says,
"The light was red."

<u>Highlight the inconsistency</u>
Q. On direct examination you said the light was green. [A: Yes]
Q. There is no question in your mind about that? [A: No question.]

<u>Lock the witness into the testimony</u> (you can omit this step)
Q. Have you ever said anything different? [No]
Q. Are you sure it was green? [Yes]
Q. Isn't it true that the light was in fact red? [No]

<u>Build up the impeaching document</u>
Q. You remember coming to my office to answer some questions?
Q. You came for a deposition on July 11, last year?
Q. I asked you questions, and you gave me answers, isn't that right?
Q. Your lawyer sat next to you while you answered?
Q. A court reporter took down your answers?
Q. That reporter gave you an oath to tell the truth?
Q. You agreed to tell the truth?
Q. After that deposition, the Q's and A's were typed up and you had a chance to read them over?
Q. After making sure it was correct, you signed it didn't you?
Q. This is your signature, isn't it?
Q. This deposition was just four months after the accident?
Q. Even though on direct examination you said that the light was green, at the deposition weren't you asked the following question, and didn't you give the following answer?
   Q: What color was the light?
   A: The light was red.

Impeachment by Inconsistent Oral Statement
(Assuming only the cross-examining lawyer heard the inconsistent statement)

Assume that although Bier testified on direct exam that "Watkins stumbled and almost fell inside the store," Bier was overheard outside the courtroom say to a person who is not available to testify, "I never really saw Watkins stumble inside the store." However, only the lawyer for Cut-Rate Liquor heard Bier's statement.

This is an inconsistent oral statement. Unlike most inconsistent statements, this one was <u>not made prior</u> to the in-court testimony on direct exam. <u>This statement was made after</u> the in-court testimony.

This fact pattern presents a special problem if the lawyer was the only person who overhead the statement. If Bier denies making the statement, the cross-examiner does not have a witness who could be called to the stand to complete the impeachment of Bier. So, if no one other that the lawyer overhead the statement, what can the lawyer do? Although no evidence rule prohibits the lawyer from testifying, rules of professional conduct in most jurisdictions would prohibit prevent the lawyer from testifying. What can the lawyer do?

Probably the best solution would be for the impeaching lawyer to be as detailed as possible during the cross leading up to the impeaching question. If the trier of fact believes the details, the trier of fact might believe that Bier also made the final statement ("I never saw him stumble inside the store.").

The detailed cross could do something like this.
Q: During the break, you went outside the courtroom, right?
Q: And you sat on the bench outside?
Q: You sat next to a man wearing a blue shirt, right?
Q: And the two of you had a conversation?
Q: You talked for about 5 minutes, right?
Q: "Even though you said on direct exam in court just 30 minutes ago that Watkins stumbled and almost fell in the store when he was at the counter, didn't you say to a man on a bench outside this courtroom just 10 minutes ago, "I never really saw Watkins stumble inside the store?"

Using Learned Treatises

FRE 803. Exceptions to the Rule Against Hearsay — Regardless of Whether the Declarant Is Available as a Witness
The following are not excluded by the rule against hearsay, regardless of whether the declarant is available as a witness:
(18) Statements in Learned Treatises, Periodicals, or Pamphlets. A statement contained in a treatise, periodical, or pamphlet if:
   (A) the statement is <u>called to the attention of an expert</u> witness on cross-examination or relied on by the expert on direct examination; and
   (B) the publication is established as a <u>reliable authority</u> by the expert's admission or testimony, by another expert's testimony, or by judicial notice.
If admitted, the statement may be <u>read</u> into evidence <u>but not received</u> as an exhibit.

> **Perspective: 38 states have a similar or identical rule;** 7 state rules only allow use of the treatise for impeachment (California, Florida, Georgia, Michigan, Oregon, Tennessee, and Virginia); 5 states have no rule (Illinois, Massachusetts, Missouri, New York, and Pennsylvania).

3 Key Points for Using the Learned Treatise

To use a learned treatise on either direct or cross-examination, under FRE 803(18)
1) there must be an expert <u>on the witness stand,</u>
2) the treatise has been established as a <u>reliable authority</u>, and
3) the statement may be <u>only read</u> into the record, but the treatise cannot be physically introduced into evidence.

Learned Treatises:
Use on Direct Exam to Support Your Expert
R803(18) – Hearsay Exception

After an expert testifies that it is not possible to determine if the plaintiff's epileptic seizures are caused by the plaintiff's auto accident, the following questioning takes place to use a learned treatise to support the expert's opinion. This is an example of using a "paper expert," or said another way, getting the opinion of two experts but only calling one as a witness.

Q: Dr. Rosenberg, are you familiar with the text called Medicine written by Dr. Mark Fishman?
A: Yes

Q: Let me show you proposed exhibit #1. What is it?
A: It is the book called Medicine written by Dr. Mark Fishman.

Q: Is it a recognized as a reliable authority in the field of medicine?
A: Yes

Q: What does the Fishman text say about the causes of epileptic seizures?
A: On page 135, Fishman says that a cause is found for seizures in less than 25% of the cases.

Using a learned treatise as a hearsay exception can <u>only done by reading</u> the treatise to the trier of fact, but <u>not by physically introducing</u> the treatise into evidence. FRE 803(18)

Learned Treatises:
Use on Cross to Attack the Opposing Expert
FRE 803(18) – Hearsay Exception

After establishing that Mark Fishman's text called "Medicine" is a reliable authority in the field of medicine, either by your expert, or by your opponent's expert, or by judicial notice (Note: judges seldom take such judicial notice), the lawyer below uses the learned treatise on cross examination to contradict the opposing party's expert witness. A statement in a treatise can be used to impeach the opponent's expert and as substantive evidence (meaning for the truth of the statement – this is a hearsay exception).

Q: Dr. Barron, you testified during your direct examination that Mr. Fulbright's epilepsy was caused by the auto accident, right?
A: Yes.

Q: Dr., there is no medical evidence that Mr. Fulbright showed any clinical evidence of brain injury immediately after the incident is there?
A: That's correct.

Q: And no evidence of a skull fracture?
A: That's also correct.

Q: And no evidence of bloody spinal fluid, right?
A: Correct again.

Q: Dr., doesn't the text called, Medicine, written by Mark Fishman, indicate on page 132 that the four symptoms most commonly found with epileptic seizures are 1) loss of consciousness, 2) clinical evidence of brain injury immediately after the incident, 3) skull fracture, and 4) bloody spinal fluid?
A: Yeah, Fishman does say that.

Q: Your Honor, no further questions.

Voicemail, Phone Conversations, Recorded Phone Conversations

There is nothing special about the identification of a telephone call. Authentication for voice identification is covered in FRE 901(b)(5)&(6).

Do you know X?

How do you know X?

How long have you known X?

Have you ever spoken with X on the phone?

How often have you spoken with X on the phone?

On [the day in question] did you have a phone conversation with X?

Who initiated that call?

[If **your** witness initiated the call]

    How did you make the call? [Ans: used contacts list on my cell phone; used recent call list on cell phone; used landline]

    Was their name already in your cell phone from previous calls to them?

    Did you recognize the voice when your call was answered?

    Who were you talking to?

(Continued on next page)

[If the **other party** initiated the call]

    Could you tell who was calling you?

    How could you tell who was calling you? [Name appeared on my cell phone]

    Why did their name appear in your cell phone? [I had name in my contacts list from many previous calls]

    Who was on the phone when you answered the call? [The defendant]

    How did you know that? [We have talked many times before. I recognized his voice.]

What did he say during that call?

Digital Evidence
Electronically Stored Information – ESI

Electronically Stored Information (EIS) includes emails, text messages, websites, fax, social media, computer printouts, and other digital records. Although evidence professors will tell you that the classic rules of evidence, created long before cell phones, computers, and the Internet, are more than adequate for the new digital world, some people may doubt it.

Yet truly, introducing digital evidence in court still does apply the same basic "HARROWing" principles found in all evidence codes – whether introducing physical items or digital evidence.

"HARROWing" is my mnemonic to remind us of evidence principles to consider when introducing physical pieces of evidence, especially physical evidence with words on or in it. HARROWing - defined as extremely distressing, agonizing, excruciating, torturing, painful, and causing physical or psychological pain – is how many new lawyers describe their experience trying to introduce evidence

H = Hearsay; FRE 800s
A= Authentication; FRE 900s
R= FRE R401 relevancy (sometime called "logical relevancy);
R= FRE403 (sometimes called "legal Relevancy);
OW = FRE 1000s Original Writings (traditionally known as Best Evidence).

The same rules of evidence apply to ESI as they do to paper and physical evidence. The most challenging foundational issues for digital evidence are establishing:1) who created the digital evidence (the author), and 2) has it been altered?

A Variety of Standards
Different standards have developed in various jurisdictions for authenticating digital evidence.

The <u>Texas courts, and probably most jurisdictions</u>, use an authentication standard identical to the standard used for traditional forms of evidence – "<u>evidence sufficient to support a finding</u> (R 901). The Texas standard can be thought of and remembered by the state's placement on a map – it is a lower standard.

However, the Maryland courts, and a few others, have developed a higher standard – like Maryland's placement on a map. Maryland courts seem to require that the proponent of digital evidence prove that the digital evidence has not been altered or hacked, it comes from a certain source, and that no one other than the owner could have used the electronic device to send or post the message. This view of EIS authentication is concerned about "voodoo information taken from the Internet." It creates a standard that can seldom be met. However, in more recent cases Maryland courts have backed away from that high standard and seem now to favor a more traditional approach for authenticating digital evidence.

The Grimm, Joseph & Capra article, Best Practices for Authenticating Digital Evidence 69 Baylor L.Rev. 1 (2017) is a great source for understanding factors in authenticating digital evidence. That article presents an overview of how FRE 104(a) and 104(b) interact in the authentication process and the article argues that digital evidence should be authenticated requiring only evidence

"sufficient to support a finding," - which is a low standard.

The authors offer the opinion that,

> "Generally speaking, it will be a rare case in which an item of digital evidence cannot be authenticated."

The article covers various ways to authenticate digital evidence. Most helpful will be the examples of various types of circumstantial evidence that would qualify as "distinctive characteristics" under FRE 901(b)(4). Additional, less frequently used methods of authenticating evidence are also covered, such as, personal knowledge of a witness, business records (in some email situations), jury comparison, and production in discovery.

Distinctive Characteristics and Circumstantial Evidence Used to Authenticate Emails and Text Messages as Having Been Sent by A Particular Person Or As Having Been Received by A Particular Person

There are many possible ways to use circumstantial evidence to qualify as "distinctive characteristics" to authenticate Electronically Stored Information (ESI) under FRE 901(b)(4) Distinctive Characteristics and the Like. Appearance, contents, substance, internal patterns, or other distinctive characteristics of the item taken together with all the circumstances are almost endless.

The Grimm, Joseph & Capra article offers many extremely valuable suggestions about circumstantial evidence which can be considered "distinctive characteristics" and used to authenticate digital evidence under R901(b)(4).

For example, when laying the foundation <u>for an email or text</u>, consider:
1) information <u>in or about</u> the email or text
2) information <u>outside</u> the email or text itself <u>that leads back to the author</u>
3) <u>forensic</u> information, and
4) information <u>outside</u> the email or text itself <u>indicating receipt of the message.</u>

Factors suggested by Grimm, Joseph, and Capra used to authenticate authorship or receipt of a message include:

1) information in or about the email or text, such as:
   - the email address, email signature, a nickname, a screen name, initials, a moniker, the author's customary use of emoji or emoticons, a writing style (including phrases and abbreviations frequently used by the author), referring to facts only the author or small group of people would know about, facts uniquely tied to the author, information about the author's family, photos of the author, items of importance to the author such as a car or a pet, and other such information

2) information outside the email or text itself that leads back to the author, such as:
- the email was part of a chain or series of emails from the same person, the claimed author told the witness to expect an email from the author, the author orally repeats its content soon after the email is sent, the author discusses the contents of the email with the third party, the author leaves a voicemail substantially of the same content, and other such information

3) forensic information, such as:
- an email's hash values or testimony from a forensic witness that the email came from a particular device at a particular time, and other such information

4) information outside the email or text itself indicating receipt of the message, such as:
- a reply was received by the sender that came from the recipient, later conduct of the recipient reflects knowledge of the contents of the sent message, later communication of the recipient reflects knowledge of the message, and the message was received and accessed on an electronic device in the possession of the recipient, and other such information.

Presenting the Digital Evidence from a Cell Phone in Court

- Print the page from the phone and use the printout in court.
- If a photo comes from a cell phone, attach the picture to an email, and then print the picture from a computer.
- Screenshot the information (picture, text message, email, social media post), email it, then print from a computer.

Self-Authentication for Digital Evidence

Recent amendments to the Federal Rules of Evidence allow for self-authentication of certified records
— See FRE 902(11)(13)(14)

Digital Evidence and Self-Authentication

FRE 902 Self-authentication
(11) Certified Domestic Records of a Regularly Conducted Activity. The original or a copy of a domestic record that meets the requirements of Rule 803(6)(A)-(C), as shown by a certification of the custodian or another qualified person that complies with a federal statute or a rule prescribed by the Supreme Court. Before the trial or hearing, the proponent must give an adverse party reasonable written notice of the intent to offer the record — and must make the record and certification available for inspection — so that the party has a fair opportunity to challenge them.

> 39 states have similar or identical rules. Many states have created forms for self-authentication of business records.

FRE 902(13) (Added to FRE Dec. 2017)
(13) Certified Records Generated by an Electronic Process or System. A record generated by an electronic process or system that produces an accurate result, as shown by a certification of a qualified person that complies with the certification requirements of Rule 902(11) or (12). The proponent must also meet the notice requirements of Rule 902(11).
   [This rule covers text messages, cell phone photos, GPS data, and other ESI]

> The following 11 states have this rule:
> Alabama, Arizona, Illinois, Iowa, Maryland, Mississippi, North Dakota, Ohio, Pennsylvania, Utah, and Wyoming

FRE 902(14) Certified Data Copied from an Electronic Device, Storage Medium, or File. Data copied from an electronic device, storage medium, or file, if authenticated by a process of digital identification, as shown by a certification of a qualified person that complies with the certification requirements of Rule 902(11) or (12). The proponent also must meet the notice requirements of Rule 902(11).

> The following 11 states have this rule:
> Alabama, Arizona, Illinois, Iowa, Maryland, Mississippi, North Dakota, Ohio, Pennsylvania, Utah, and Wyoming

Email – Witness is the Sender (Outgoing Email)

Q: How did you notify Cut-Rate about …
A: I sent an email to Dan Jones

Q: What email address did you use?
A: DJones@Cutrate.com

Q: How do you know that was the correct address?
A: He and I have email back and forth for a few months, and all of his emails to me came from that email address

Q: Let me show you what has been marked as plaintiff's proposed exhibit #1.

Q: What is it? (A printout of the email I sent to Jones that day.).

Q: How do you know that? (I wrote it. I remember it. It was in my "sent mail" folder.)

Q: Your Honor I offer the exhibit into evidence.

Email – Witness is the Recipient (Incoming Email)

Do you know Dan Jones?

How do you know him?

Are you familiar with the email address DJones@Cutrate.com?

Have you received emails from Dan Jones in the past?

Have you sent emails to Dan Jones at that address?

Has he responded to your emails from that email address?

Is that email address in your email contacts?

In late April, did you receive an email from Dan Jones about selling liquor?

Did you recognize email address as being from Dan Jones?

I am handing you what has been marked as proposed exhibit #7. Do you recognize it?

What is it? (A: The email from Dan Jones)

Why would you say that's an email from Dan Jones?
[provide information about distinctive characteristics of this email]

How did you get a paper copy of this email? (A: I printed it out.)

Is this a true and accurate printout of that email?

Your Honor, I offer the proposed exhibit into evidence.

> [The email reads: "I might be getting fired. They caught me selling booze to drunks again."]

Text Message
Received by Witness

Do you know Y?

Do you communicate with Y on a regular basis?

In what ways to you communicate with Y?

Did you receive a text message from the Y [recently; on or about _ date, on the topic of …, etc.]?

Would you recognize a printout of the message if you were to see it again?

Let me show you what has been marked as proposed exhibit # 1. Do you recognize it?

What is it? [Ans: A screenshot from my cell phone]

How do you know that this is a message from Y? [It is similar to other messages I have received from Y in that …]

How did it appear when it arrived on your phone? [Showed up under the name and with the picture I had previously assigned to Y]

What other distinctive characteristics did you notice about the message? [provide as many as distinctive characteristics possible]

Is it a fair and accurate representation of the text message you received [recently; on or about _ date, on the topic of visiting your son, etc.]?

Has it been altered in any way?

I would like to enter the proposed exhibit into evidence

Social Media
Facebook, Instagram, Snapchat, Twitter, and other Posts

Do you know B?

How long have you known him?

Are you familiar with Facebook?

Does B have a Facebook account?

Have you seen posts by B on his Facebook account in the past?

How do you know that B made those posts? [provide distinctive characteristics]

Have you seen a posting on B's Facebook account about [the matter in question]?

Let the record reflect that I am handing you what has been marked as proposed exhibit 12 and ask if you can identify it?

What is it?

Is that a screenshot of the Facebook posting by B about ___?

What day did you take the screenshot?

Is it a true and accurate screenshot of that posting?

Is the post still on B's account? [Ask this question only if it is currently on the account.]

I offer the proposed exhibit into evidence.

Laying Foundations

Internet Website – Web Posting

Did you visit Professor John Barkai's webpage? [Yes]

How did you access it? [Googled "John Barkai" on my phone]

How did you find his page?
    Ans: "Yes, I clicked on the link that said
        "Prof. John Barkai Homepage.""

What did you find when you clicked on that link for the homepage?
    Ans: I found his list of courses and other posts.

Did you click on any particular link?
    Ans: I clicked Hawaii Rules of Evidence (HRE) Book Page

What did you find on that page when you clicked on it?
      A: I found a link to buy from Amazon a copy of several
      different evidence handbooks.

Let me show you what's been marked as proposed exhibit # 14. Can
    you identify it?
      A: Yes. It's a screenshot of that webpage with instructions
      about how to buy books from Amazon.

Was that screenshot a print of the page from his website?
      A: Yes, I printed it myself.

Is this exhibit a fair and accurate copy of that webpage?   [Yes]

Has this exhibit of the screenshot been altered or otherwise change from the image on your phone in any way?   [No]

I offer the exhibit into evidence.

Fax – Incoming

Does your office have a fax machine?

Do you send outgoing faxes?

Do you receive incoming faxes?

Have you received purchase orders from the defendant by fax in the past?

Let me show you plaintiff's proposed exhibit # 27 and ask if you can identify it? [A: Yes. I can]

What is it? [A: A fax I received about six months ago from the defendant]

Why do you say this fax came from the defendant?
A: There are number of factors in addition to the document being written on the defendant's letterhead stationery. The fax is signed by the head of defendant's purchasing department, and I am familiar with her signature from our past dealings. Further, imprinted on the bottom of this fax sheet is the fax number for the defendant's company, and I have faxed prior documents to the defendant by using that number. Finally, the document relates to the purchase of some equipment that I had discussed with the defendant's head of purchasing just a few hours before the fax arrived at my office.

Is this document in the same or substantially the same condition as it was when you received it? [A: Yes, it is exactly the same.]

There have been no alterations or changes? [A: None whatsoever.]

Your Honor, I move that this proposed exhibit be admitted into evidence.

Expert Opinions

> **Georgia** uses the **Daubert** standard for **CIVIL** expert witness testimony, **see OCGA § 24-7-702,** but follows Harper v. State, 249 Ga. 519, 292 S.E.2d 389 (1982) and seems to use a different standard for **CRIMINAL** cases codified as §24-7-707

> **Admissibility of Expert Testimony.**
> The majority of states have explicitly adopted the Daubert (FRE702) standard. A minority of states use either the Frye ("general acceptance") standard or some combination of Daubert and Frye standards. Additionally, "general acceptance" is part of the Daubert standard.

Four Part Expert Opinion Foundation and Testimony

1. Elicit the <u>background and qualifications</u> of the expert
2. Tender or offer the witness as expert in a particular field
   (e.g., 'general medicine.")
   – Opponent is allowed to voir dire (test qualifications by cross examination limited to the expert's qualifications, but not the facts of this case)
3. <u>Offer the expert's opinion</u> or conclusion (to a particular standard such as "reasonable medical certainty") FRE 702
4. <u>Offer the basis for opinion</u> FRE703
   – Including reasonable reliance on inadmissible evidence
   – Disclosure of inadmissible evidence?

Three Simple Questions

1) Q: "Do you have an opinion as to whether…
2) Q: "What is that opinion?"
3) Q: "How did you reach that opinion?
   A: [including inadmissible information reasonably relied upon by experts in the particular field, FRE 703]

How to Start
The expert witness examination normally starts with questions to establish the witness' qualifications to testify as an expert.

Topics for Background and Qualifications of an Expert:
- formal education, work experience, number of previous times retained, qualified, and testified as an expert, in which courts, on-the-job training, non-degree training courses, publications in the field, teaching in the field, memberships in related professional associations, and any other topics relevant to showing the person is an expert.

Tender / Offer
After presenting the expert's background and qualifications, in jurisdictions where the judge must "certify" or "find" that the witness is an expert and is to permitted to testify as an expert, the lawyer presenting the expert then "tenders" or "offers" the witness to the judge as an expert, stating the field of expertise.

"I offer/tender Mr. X as an expert in the field of…"

"I ask the court to certify Ms. Y as an expert in the field of …"

Can you call the expert an "expert?"
After any voir dire (a limited cross examination to test the qualifications of the witness) by opposing counsel and objections, the judge rules on whether the expert can continue to testify as an expert. Some courts do not allow the lawyer to use the word "expert" to refer to the expert witness. but the judge is still changed with the responsibility of determining if the witness is qualified as an expert. Yet no one uses the word "expert" in front of lay fact finders. The apparent reason for such a practice is, as explained below.

The 2000 Advisory Committee Notes to the amendment to Federal Rule of Evidence 702 says, in part:

"…The use of the term "expert" in the Rule does not, however, mean that a jury should actually be informed that a qualified witness is testifying as an "expert." Indeed, there is much to be said for a practice that prohibits the use of the term "expert" by both the parties and the court at trial. Such a practice "ensures that trial courts do not inadvertently put their stamp of authority" on a witness's opinion, and protects against the jury's being "overwhelmed by the so-called 'experts'.""

More Tenders/Offers of the expert
"We believe that Mr. Taylor should be permitted to offer his opinions in this case."

"I tender Dr. Barron as an expert in the field of family medicine and request that she be allowed to testify as such.

"I offer Dr. Rosenberg as an expert in the field of neurology."

"Judge, we ask that the court accept Dr. Shigeta as an expert in civil engineering."

Offering the Opinion
Traditionally, the opinion is delivered in a two-question sequence:
> Q1: Do you have an opinion as ....?
> A: Yes
> Q2: What is that opinion?

"Do you have an opinion, within a reasonable degree of scientific certainty, as to the time of death of Ms. X?"

"Do you have an opinion, to a reasonable degree of medical probability, as to whether the motorcycle accident caused Mr. Fulbright's epilepsy?"

"Do you have an opinion, to a reasonable degree of engineering certainty, as to whether the XXX caused the bridge to fail?"

"Do you have an opinion whether Mr. X suffered a brain damage as a result of the fight?"

Standards for Stating an Expert's Opinion
There are no minimum standards under FRE 702 describing how "good" an expert's opinion must be to be stated in court. By case law, some courts and jurisdictions require that the standard must be stated to a
> "reasonable degree of [medical] certainty," or a
> "reasonable degree of [scientific] probability."

Other jurisdictions simply allow an expert to state an opinion without any specific qualification.
> "What did your examination reveal?"

The above standards of "certainty" and "probability" are vague and rather unhelpful standards to a lay jury or courts-martial member who might be able to understand percentages, but who are given no guidance to the certainty or probability. Do those standards mean 51%, 65%, 75%, 85%, 95%, etc.? "Preponderance of the evidence" does have an associated percentage (50%+), but terms such as "sufficient to support a finding," "clear and convincing," "beyond a reasonable doubt," as well as "certainty" and "probability" do not. Simply, use whatever standard your judge and jurisdiction require. In an attempt to be persuasive, some lawyers ask the experts questions like:

"How positive are you of your opinion?"
"What is the degree of your certainty?"

Inadmissible Information Reasonably Relied Upon

Experts can base their opinions on hearsay and other inadmissible evidence. FRE 703 says in part:

> "If experts in the particular field would reasonably rely on those kinds of facts or data in forming an opinion on the subject, they need not be admissible for the opinion to be admitted."

You should have in your tool chest of questions this question. <u>"Is that the type of information reasonably relied upon by experts in your field?"</u>

Remember

Whoever has the Biggest, Most Qualified Expert Might Win

Because opposing parties usually present opposing experts who have reached opposing conclusions, the advocacy principle is for you to try to present a more qualified and more credible expert than your opponent's expert. If "your" expert's testimony and conclusions are believed on the issue in dispute, you are more likely to win your case.

Books by John Barkai

Federal Rules of Evidence Handbook with Common Objections & Evidentiary Foundations

Humor in Negotiations & ADR: Cartoon Caption Contest Winners from the ABA Dispute Resolution Magazine

Humor in Trial Evidence: Cartoon Caption Contest Winners and Challenges from My Evidence Class

Military Rules of Evidence Handbook with Common Objections & Evidentiary Foundations

Negotiation and Mediation Communication Gambits for Breaking Impasses and More: What Do I Say When I Want To ...

The Pocket Guide to Common Trial Objections & Evidentiary Foundations

The following evidence books (for all 50 states and many other jurisdictions) in my Handbooks with Common Objections & Evidentiary Foundations series are available exclusively on Amazon for the following states:

Alabama	Idaho	Missouri	Pennsylvania **
Alaska	Illinois	Montana	Rhode Island
Arizona	Indiana	Nebraska	South Carolina
Arkansas	Iowa	Nevada	South Dakota
California **	Kansas	New Hampshire	Tennessee
Colorado	Kentucky	New Jersey	Texas **
Connecticut	Louisiana	New Mexico	Utah
Delaware	Maine **	New York	Vermont
District of Columbia	Maryland	North Carolina	Virginia
Florida **	Massachusetts	North Dakota	Washington
Georgia	Michigan **	Ohio	West Virginia
Hawaii **	Minnesota	Oklahoma	Wisconsin
	Mississippi	Oregon	Wyoming
Pacific Island countries and other U.S. affiliated jurisdictions			
American Samoa		Northern Mariana Islands	
Chuuk		Pohnpei	
Federated States of Micronesia		Puerto Rico	
Guam		Republic of Palau	
Kosrae		U.S. Virgin Islands	
Marshall Islands		Yap	

** I also published "Just the Rules" books for these seven states.

Massachusetts, Missouri, and New York do not have formal rules of evidence, but Massachusetts and New York do publish state "Guides" to evidence

To find John Barkai's evidence and cartoon books

1. Go to the Amazon website – www.Amazon.com

2. Enter into the search bar: - John Barkai

3. For a particular state, enter into the Amazon search bar
   - John Barkai [state name]

The books are available exclusively on Amazon.com and are "print-on-demand."

History and Restyling of the Federal Rules of Evidence

The Federal Rules of Evidence (FRE) were adopted in 1975. Approximately 46 states have adopted evidence codes, by statute or court rule, which are patterned on the FRE. The states without FRE based evidence codes are California, Kansas, Missouri, and New York. The California Evidence Code took effect in 1965 and is quite different in structure than any other state evidence code.

Although most states modeled their evidence rules after the FRE, almost every state has some evidence provisions which are different from the federal rules and some states have very significant differences.

The FRE were "restyled" in 2011 to
> "make them more easily understood and to make style and terminology consistent throughout the rules. These changes are intended to be stylistic only. There is no intent to change any result in any ruling on evidence admissibility.... The [Restyling] Committee made special efforts to reject any purposed style improvement that might result in a substantive change in the application of a rule." --- See Restyled Rules Committee Note for Restyled Rules of Evidence.

So far, at least thirteen (13) states, have restyled their rules of evidence: Arizona (2012), Delaware (2017), Idaho (2018), Indiana (2013), Iowa (2017), Maine (2015), Mississippi (2016), New Hampshire (2017), Pennsylvania (2013), South Dakota (2016), Texas (2014), Utah (2012), and West Virginia (2014). The Military (2013) and the Commonwealth of the Northern Mariana Islands (2015) have also restyled.

An excellent resource for understanding the differences between the FRE and the evidence rules of other states is the multi-volume treatise, Wharton's Criminal Evidence by Bergman and Hollander. This treatise is available in many law libraries and is available on Westlaw, where it is called CRIMEVID database. Despite included the word "Criminal" in its title, the treatise discusses evidence issues (criminal and civil) but does not cover FRE 407, 408, and 411, and it does not cover the criminal topic of confrontation.

Dedication

To my wife Linda and my adult twin daughters Hope and Leah,
who bring me so much joy and enrich my life
and
to the hundreds of my former evidence and clinical students
who learned these rules of evidence with me
over the past 50 years
at the William S. Richardson School of Law
at the University of Hawaii
and
Wayne State Law School in Detroit.

About the Author

John Barkai has been teaching evidence since 4 B.C. – that is 4 years "Before Computers" were used at the University of Hawaii Law School. His major criminal trial practice experience was in 1972-1973 in Detroit, and included jury trials on charges for Murder, Criminal Sexual Conduct (then called Statutory Rape), Armed Robbery, Assault, and CCW (Carrying A Concealed Weapon). He did not use the federal rules of evidence at that time. No one did. The Federal Rules did not go into effect until July 1975, by which time he was a fulltime law professor.

Professor Barkai is a former Detroit Michigan criminal trial lawyer, a fulltime law professor for 50 years - a Professor of Law at the William S. Richardson School of Law at the University of Hawaii for 45 years and taught at Wayne State University for 5 years. He has taught evidence since 1981 and has been the Director, and now Co-Director, of the Law School's Clinical Program since 1978. He has been a member of the Hawaii Supreme Court's Standing Committee on the Rules of Evidence since 1993. He has a B.B.A, M.B.A, and J.D, all from the University of Michigan. For the past 50 years, he has taught a criminal clinic in which his students try traffic and minor criminal cases under the state student practice rule. This handbook, and other similar handbooks, were inspired by handbooks he created in 2019 for a workshop for Pacific Island Judges from American Samoa, Marshall Islands, Federated States of Micronesia, Chuuk, Kosrae, Pohnpei, and Yap. He has published evidence handbooks similar to this one for all 50 states as well as 15 other jurisdictions from American Samoa to the U.S. Virgin Islands. He also has evidence and negotiation & ADR cartoon books on Amazon as well as a book on effective communication for negotiation and mediation.

Made in the USA
Coppell, TX
20 July 2023